A WRITER'S ROAD MAP

By

WENDELL WELLMAN

ISBN: 1-4033-8751-6 (e-book)
ISBN: 1-4033-8752-4 (Paperback)

Library of Congress Control Number: 2002095294

This book is printed on acid free paper.

Printed in the United States of America
Bloomington, IN

1stBooks – rev. 10/24/02

TABLE OF CONTENTS

FOREWORD

Throughout my career as a professional screenwriter, I have been asked to talk about writing at numerous story groups and seminars. There is one moment during these evenings that I can always count on. When we enter the forest of pure plot, everybody gets excited. There is confusion, there is excitement, there is hunger.

Everybody has great ideas. A lot of us have talent in developing quirky characters and great dialogue; but plot construction is the great Enemy. As writers, we are thrust into a deep forest that we are expected to find our way out of. So how do we do this? Is there a secret, magical prototype buried out there? The answer is that there are numerous hidden prototypes. They are not written down. They are rarely presented in classes. They are not spelled out.

As writers we are expected to create a progression of many scenes . . . that paint a picture, that work as allegory, that chart an emotional journey within. How do we do this? Where do we look for a blueprint? How do we know that this sequence should be here, and another sequence should be there?

My book focuses on plot construction. I have worked with other writers in collaborations. Invariably, we will find ourselves up against it. Our discussions are always about plot problems. "We haven't solved this section. What do we do about the middle section? Do we take this pathway or that?"

The longer I write, the more I appreciate the discoveries that I have made. Recently, one young writer said to me, "I was giving up writing. This gives me hope."

Ultimately this is what story telling is in its simplest form, isn't it? You create characters in bondage. You give them hope. This is a chronicle of my own twenty years of searching for hope. This is a how-to book that offers you a road map.

CHAPTER 1 ·

SCREENWRITING FROM THE TRENCHES

I am a professional writer. So are a few of my friends. Each one of us has sold a screenplay; each of us has sold more than one. Each of us has had a movie produced. Each of us has made great money at times. Yet, we all still struggle with the process of writing. I have one pal who has had three studio movies produced, and yet he is still lost in the middle of his latest screenplay.

This book is a result of hundreds of hours of story sessions, plot discussions, and "in the trenches" late night, loss of sleep, writer paranoia . . .

I have begun to build a model for myself. I use it. Writer partners that I collaborate with use it. When I read my pals' screenplays, I use it. When they analyze my screenplays, they use it. It helps us. It gives us a common language. So, whatever section of the screenplay we are struggling with, we know how to talk about it.

There are a few heady ideas in the model. But mostly, it is a model for you to build a story. It offers you a section-by-section breakdown of storytelling. You may find it doesn't work for you. In other words, you may have a story to tell, and you may not need this information. But, if you get lost somewhere in the writing, you can pick up this book and you can refer to the map. It should be helpful as it is an attempt to show you the order that is best for the story sections or beats, for example. Will you use every beat in your story? Of course not, but if you treat this as a good working model, it will help you to make your plot read like a professional. Then when you get your foot in the door, an agent will take you seriously.

Now, when I give out a new screenplay of mine to agents or producers they may not always buy it, but they always give me this note: "Very professional, a solid, well-constructed story with good characters." I didn't always get that note in the past. Sometimes I would get the note: "The story got lost somewhere," or the classic, "I didn't get it."

I have made progress. This book is an attempt to provide a shortcut to you so you can take advantage of the progress that I have made.

WHY THIS BOOK?

There is an explosion of writing technology books hitting the marketplace. Big name writing gurus, world-class lecturers, and teachers from some of our most prestigious film schools. I've read many of these books, hungry for some answers as to why the middle of my screenplays were falling apart. The problem is, I wasn't getting technical answers to my problems from any of these books. So I started watching successful movies over and over. I began to recognize certain motifs and movie sections that appear at certain points in movies . . . in every movie. This is how I began to form a map.

Once you have been writing for a while, it is the middle section that begins to kill you. When my pals give me their screenplays for notes, it is the middle sections that are killing them. I occasionally teach screenwriting classes around Hollywood. Invariably, a student will pay me to give notes on his or her screenplay. Again, the problem is, you guessed it, the middle section. The one piece of good news for you is that within my circle of successful writer pals, we all had less trouble in the middle section when we first started writing. We were writing on instinct then. One of my pals said to me recently, "Maybe we only have one or two stories in us." I didn't say anything but basically, I don't agree with him. I think I would rather go back to my years of training as an actor for the explanation. There is a cliché axiom around acting circles. "You can get by on instinct in your first couple of roles. But after that, you had better develop some craft."

I have had some high points. I am thinking back to a moment on the set of Clint Eastwood's *Sudden Impact*. It was a night shoot on the boardwalk in Santa Cruz. I was there to play the role of "Tyrone," a great part, one of the main bad guys in the movie. But, due to a complicated set of circumstances, Eastwood was also allowing me to do some rewrites of some scenes, even though this was not my screenplay.

I spent three days in my hotel room, writing the scenes. I turned them in to the production offices. Next, I was standing there in wardrobe, reporting for work as an actor. A huge crowd of spectators were standing behind the barricade. It was a big deal for the people of Santa Cruz to see Dirty Harry. But, my heart was pounding. "Maybe he hated my stuff," I thought. Suddenly, Eastwood finished a take and walked over to me. He said, "I read the pages. I like it. We are going to shoot it all." He then proceeded to give me another scene to work on for the night shoot.

It was one of the highlights of my career. I had already co-written *Firefox* for Eastwood with my partner, Alex Lasker. I was once again writing for Eastwood, and doing a featured role as an actor at the same time. Eastwood later brought me on to rewrite another movie for him. Warner Brothers gave me a two-picture deal. I figured the winds of destiny were blowing my way . . .

I have had my low points . . . I am thinking of a time that I was sitting in the office of the production chief at Warner Brothers. I had just lost a WGA arbitration to Sylvester Stallone on the movie, *Cobra.* Every writer loses an WGA arbitration sooner or later. It is almost a badge of courage in this town. The production chief tried to assuage me, "You will be doing other projects at Warners." I was still upset. I was paid by the studio to develop the screenplay. I was the original writer.

Privately, I knew why I was upset. It wasn't this movie. I had read Stallone's rewrite of my screenplay. It wasn't good. *Cobra* was going to be a bad movie. And the book that I had adapted, *Fair Game,* was a mediocre book to begin with. What was really upsetting was the realization that I was going to be thrust back into the forest of plot. *Firefox* and *Fair Game* were books. It's not that difficult to adapt a book. *Sudden Impact* was already a screenplay. Now I was going to have to rejoin the workforce. I was going to have to create entire screenplays from my head. In other words, I was going to be facing the Enemy, plot construction, head on . . . again.

I have been fighting this Enemy for years. Sometimes I would rebel against writing. The constraints of screenwriting structure would become so confining, I would simply stop. I wrote plays as an act of rebellion. I had my plays produced. It was fun. But all the while, the phantom of the visual movie story beckoned me. I missed the forest. I couldn't go to the movies as just a fan. My mind was continually studying each writer's structure. I would appreciate a good decision; I would note a bad one. I would still be working, even though I was sitting in the theater to be entertained. Like I said, I missed the forest. Movie storytelling is like no other storytelling that we know. It is a succession, an explosion of images. It is closer to a fever dream than anything else. It is a challenge that continues to intoxicate.

This book is a chronicle of my ongoing war. I have become a student of films. To be a screenwriter, you must be a student of films. Every time you walk into a movie theater, you are in the classroom.

So I return to my question, why this book? This is more of a down and dirty "in the trenches" approach to the craft of writing. It is a how-to book from a writer who is currently writing, a writer who is succeeding and failing, and a group of writer pals who are succeeding and failing. It is an attempt to put a model on paper . . . step-by-step, section-by-section . . . that we try to work with. Think of this as a path through the forest, a writer's road map. It is not the only way. There are many ways. Again, the lesson you are already beginning to learn is the more you write on instinct in the beginning, the better off you are.

This book is deliberately short and deliberately less intellectual than most of the books on the market. Some of those other books are terrific; some of the teachers are terrific. I recommend that you study with them if you have the opportunity. This is not an attempt to compete because my approach is different.

I am working from the premise that you want to write now. You want to read this book in a few hours, pick up a couple of "killer" techniques, and watch a couple of videos. Then, you want to hit the keyboard. Consider this guerilla screenwriting. I am giving you a road map. This is screenwriting from the trenches.

WATCHING MOVIES

Let me share a couple of personal stories. When I first began to write, I got very lucky. I wrote with a partner, Alex Lasker. We were roommates in college. Now, here we are five years after graduation, writing together. And, getting paid to write right out of the box! We had our ups and downs, believe me. I'll be sharing some of our experiences in this book. But the point is, we were writing on instinct. We had no training. What we did was watch movies. Later, our writing partnership dissolved. We both went on to solo writing careers. But, we both continue to watch movies.

I remember one particular evening that I think is very funny. I live in Santa Monica. Most of my writing pals also live in this area. The Third Street Promenade is the place where everyone goes to see first-run pictures. One particular Sunday evening, I decided to take in a late show. The movie playing was *The Usual*

Suspects. I purchased my ticket and Diet Coke and walked into the darkened theatre. There were maybe ten people in the huge, spacious theatre. I thought, "Perfect, my kind of night." I had the entire left section to myself. I saw one man sitting down front. He had a whole section to himself. The trailers ended and the movie began. Suddenly, the man looked around. He was one of my writer pals. He saw me. He acted a little embarrassed but waved. I waved back. Within a couple of minutes, I noticed another one of my writer pals. He was sitting in the center section, a little to the rear of me. He looked over and waved. We all continued to watch the movie. None of us said hello or socialized afterwards. We didn't call each other later to joke about it. We were there to do business.

Watching movies, studying how fellow artists apply the craft, is flat out the best way to learn. It is doing business. I have made a conscious choice to support every concept that I discuss with you, every section of our story, with movie illustrations.

If it seems a little like "Ebert and Friends" at the movies at times, so be it. Referencing movies while you are discussing the craft just seems to work. You can talk about concepts all day, but seeing is getting it. I try to explain my illustrations clearly enough so that you can get it in the book. However, if you want to have more fun, I suggest that you pick up three videos—that's all, and watch them with your partner. Try to see if you can recognize the ideas we are talking about in the videos.

I have chosen some deliberately lightweight, audience-friendly Hollywood movies. Trust me, I prefer the more complex, structurally challenging movies to watch. But I have learned over the years that by limiting myself to the cerebral, art-house cinema that I prefer, I was also limiting my learning curve. The weird thing is that I have learned more about the holes in my craft from some of the superficial comedies and movies that I really don't like than from anywhere else. Why? Because the conflicts are simple and the shifts are obvious. It is easy to see the sections. I have learned that when I need to examine the difficult areas of writing, such as inner conflict or midpoint shift, it is easy to see. At the same time, throughout the book, I will also discuss some of the films that I think are great and structurally challenging as well.

Let me give you one more personal experience. There is a group of people who meet once a month at Sony Studios in Hollywood. The group is called "Storyboard." It is a great group and resource for writers. Most of the group consists of writers or producers. Some of them are lawyers or schoolteachers. But they all share love of the craft of writing. The group invites me as a moderator several times a year. My job is to help analyze a screenplay or a new movie that is about to open. The discussions get wild and they get heated. I like it . . . I always put up my model, which you will see later, on the blackboard. It helps me to articulate the different sections of the movie. But, here is the discovery I have made. Sometimes when we are discussing a particularly difficult idea, I sometimes get tongue-tied. My face gets red and I feel the sweat droplets forming on my brow. I find myself frustrated and asking, "do you see what I am saying?" Some people are agreeing, but others are just staring at me. In desperation, I start reeling off examples from two or three movies that everybody has seen. "Did everybody see *Pay It Forward?* It is this scene. Did everybody see *The Sixth Sense?* It is this scene. Did everybody see *Boogie Nights?* It is this scene!" Suddenly, everybody is nodding their heads. The group gets excited. Now we are all speaking the same language. Now we can return to the same kind of scene in the movie of the evening.

This is a discovery that I made out of desperation. If you are talking about something as difficult as the "two ways of thinking," for example, it is easier to explain it with several examples. If you discuss the idea first, and then give a couple of movie examples back to back . . . it is easier to get it. By the way, I also use this method personally. I will decide that one area of my writing is weak. I will then go to the movies for a month, and just concentrate on that area only in each movie. I will come home and keep a running log of how each movie handled the area. I will study the log at least once a week. "Okay, this movie did it this way, that movie did it this way, and that movie did it that way." It helps me to understand.

A FINAL THOUGHT...
BEFORE OUR ADVENTURE

I make a consistent point in this book regarding the architecture of plot. You can use all kinds of creative devices in storytelling. You can have multiple, protagonists, which is au currant, *Boogie Nights, Pulp Fiction, Your Friends and Neighbors, Go.* You can retell the same story or incident from multiple points of view, *The Usual Suspects.* You can twist and distort time, *Pulp Fiction.* Or, you can tell three completely separate stories simultaneously, *Traffic.* But there is a mandatory requirement for your plot to be successful. Whether you are using one Hero or three Heroes, each Hero must have his own Enemy. And your plot requires a minimum number of encounters, engagements, or battles between your Hero and your Enemy.

Please don't let this term confuse you. In my road map, I label them battles. At other times, I label them engagements. Sometimes I even refer to them as puzzles or tests. In each case, I am talking about the same thing . . . a conflict scene. A scene in which your Hero and his Enemy are engaging each other, struggling with each other, trying to learn to love each other, dueling with each other, fighting over the prize. The reason I have chosen to use multiple labels for these Hero and Enemy scenes is that I don't believe any one label does these scenes justice. Because, your job as the writer is to create fresh and different engagements each time your Hero and Enemy meet.

William Shakespeare was a master of this. In *Hamlet,* our Hero, the Prince of Denmark, had one true Enemy, Claudius, his stepfather, the King. The basic device at work is Hamlet's "madness." He feigned madness; this allowed him to slip in verbal jabs. He could probe at Claudius without consequences. Later, he staged a mock play with a group of traveling players. Hamlet studied Claudius. He created a puzzle. He tried to trap Claudius in his guilt.

But, notice that this scene presents a deepening conflict within Hamlet. If he implicated Claudius in this scene, he would also implicate Gertrude, his mother. And, Hamlet had a whole consort of Oedipal and rage issues with Gertrude. Look what else happened in this scene. Hamlet was ambivalent towards Ophelia at best. But, suddenly, Hamlet was all man. He became sexually aggressive.

These are two separate engagements or battles between Hamlet and his Enemy. "Madness," and then a play. Notice how different the battles are. Notice the progression in the level of conflicts between the first battle and the second battle. This is what I am encouraging you to do in your writing. Come up with fresh and different encounters between the Hero and Enemy each time they meet. This is why I use different labels for these scenes throughout the book.

So often when I receive screenplays from friends or students, the adventure begins well. For example, there is a murder in the neighborhood. The Hero is a working class single Mom. She decides to solve the murder. She finds the Killer at a bar. She begins to follow him. But here is the trap most writers fall into . . . She keeps following him! There is a chase scene. There is more following him. Wrong! You get the picture. There is no progression. The story is going nowhere. You can't learn much about your Enemy by following him.

A WORD OF ADVICE: Avoid multiple Heroes in your first screenplay. Don't try to play games with time or shifting points of view. Save these tricks for a later screenplay. Even among my writer pals, we agree on this. You have to tell a simple story first. Later on, maybe, you can go back and play some games with your story . . . chop off the first act for example, start in the middle of things. Avoid this for now. Choose one Hero, present him with an Adventure. Give him one complex, wildly challenging opponent. Look for rich characters to accompany your Hero on his journey. That is a challenging enough assignment. Or, as they say in writing circles, "Keep it simple, stupid."

CHAPTER 2

STORYTELLING

THE KITCHEN TABLE— HOW TO GET STARTED

Every one of you out there has a story in you. You know you do. How many times have you been hanging with friends, and one of you is telling something funny that happened. You are in a restaurant; there are four of you. The laughter is so big at your table, the entire restaurant is beginning to stare. But you guys don't care. Every one of you adds a bit to the story. This story is a winner. Guaranteed howls every time. Suddenly your friend grabs your arm, and both of you say it . . . "This should be a movie." It's best to work with somebody. Maybe it is the friend who grabbed your arm at the restaurant and said, "This is a movie." Two minds are usually better than one.

There was an article in the *Los Angeles Times*. It was about two young men who live in Orange County, California. One guy had a job in a video store and he lived with his mom. The other guy didn't have a job. But he had a sleeping bag and he was willing to sleep on his friend's floor. The *Times* interviewed the mom and the two young men. Our two Heroes dedicated six months to writing in that bedroom or at the kitchen table. They had never written before. They had never taken a writing class. They just believed and were willing to commit. Their screenplay sold for a MILLION DOLLARS. There are many stories like

13

this. You can do it. Remember something, I partnered up with a UCLA chum, Alex Lasker. We wrote our first screenplay without ever taking a screenwriting class. We certainly didn't understand these concepts. But, we sold our first screenplay. This screenplay led to our second screenplay, a paid writing assignment at Paramount pictures, with Michael Eisner, Jeff Katzenburg, and the late Don Simpson as our bosses. Wow! A pretty rarified atmosphere for a couple of young writers who had never studied writing. Neither of our first two screenplays got produced. However, Clint Eastwood happened to read our second screenplay and offered us the *Firefox* assignment. So our third screenplay was a "go" picture. So now we have some work to do. We need to define what a story is.

A SIMPLE PROTOTYPE

You give your Hero a crisis. He needs money. He needs it in forty-eight hours. Or, the boyfriend leaves our lady Hero abandoned in a small town. She has no money. What is she going to do to survive? Whatever the situation, think of it as a puzzle, a maze, a tight spot. You plan your plot. Is our Hero going to find his or her way out? The Hero will face three or four, or more, different obstacles or tests. You create an Enemy, or several Enemies. Their job is to keep frustrating or defeating the Hero within these obstacles or tests. Your Enemies should start piling on defeat after defeat. Eventually the Hero faces the most difficult test. It is a moment of intense suffering. This is a death scene. But the Hero gains new insight here. The Hero is broken, but he or she is becoming a new person. The Hero is ready to solve the puzzle. The Hero is ready to find freedom. This is a simple prototype. And, it really works for me. Whenever I get lost in plotting, I try to go back and review this model. It helps me.

In this book, we are going to work with the major elements in storytelling, step by step. We start with your idea, a question that you want to answer. We pick a Hero. We pick an Enemy. We examine how the movie starts in the normal world. We pick friends who will have similar adventures. We examine the tests, or battles. We will discuss how several of these big tests or battles need to shift the direction of your story. We will discuss some of the more subtle devices you can use in your story. Building inner conflict for your Hero, for example. Or finding a controlling symbol. But in the end, you don't need to get intimidated or overwhelmed. Just keep reminding yourself that storytelling is simple. You create a Hero. You give him a puzzle, a maze; you put him in a tight spot. You create three or four major tests, or obstacles, that the Hero must face. You create an Enemy or Enemies. The Enemy's job is to defeat the Hero in these tests. He needs to pile on the defeats . . . If you keep returning to this simple prototype, you can't go wrong. You are on your way to writing a good story.

JASON AND THE GOLDEN FLEECE

A few years ago, I picked up a simple book on Greek legends. At least once a year, I reread the stories of Perseus, Hercules, and Jason the Argonaut. Why? It helps to remind me of how simple storytelling should be. It gives me a plot structure in big bold colors. There is always a family crisis in the beginning of these stories. Usually, the Hero is banished from the homeland because an uncle or another bad relative has seized the throne. So it is a family problem, and a question of the rights to kingship. In Jason's case, it is Uncle Pelias who is king, and fears Jason. The Hero is then sent on an impossible quest. He needs to do this to save himself, or his mother, or some other family member. In the case of Jason and the Argonauts, Pelias the King sends Jason off to a far country to retrieve the Golden Fleece. All of these stories have a similar structure. In the legend of *Perseus,* for example, Perseus must protect his mother, Danae, from the evil advances of King Polydectes. So Perseus is sent off on a journey to do the impossible, to cut off the heads of the Gorgon. So returning to Jason and the Argonauts, Jason must leave Iolcos, his normal world, and journey to strange and exotic places. He must face one difficult task after another. Jason and his men must fight off the Harpies. They must risk their ship against the crashing rocks of the Straits of Bosphorus. Now Jason finds himself face to face with another evil monarch, Aeetes, King of the Colchians. Aeetes gives Jason more "sure death" assignments before he will surrender the Golden Fleece. Jason now must take on the giant bulls, an army of giants that rise out of the ground, a monstrous serpent that keeps watch over the Fleece.

As I watch a lot of movies, I have begun to realize that this is structure. You give your Hero a crisis. You send him on a journey. Psychologically, you need to see your Hero suffer through test after test, one test bigger and more exotic than the next . . . Eventually, we, as an audience, become as weary and battle scarred as our Hero. The Hero is winning, but he is not winning. The Evil King is still in control. We are ready for the Hero to change. Aeetes has a beautiful daughter, Medea. She falls in love with Jason on sight. He falls in love with Medea. This is the love interest. And it happens in the middle of the story. Medea is a goddess and she has magical powers that Jason needs. But, this sets up a deeper conflict for Jason. If he takes Medea with him, he is inviting the wrath of Aeetes. Jason decides to take his ladylove with him on the quest. Watch how many movies build a second level of conflict with the beautiful female protagonist. Medea faces her own conflict; she must choose family or her new love. Eventually, both Heroes will face consequences for their illicit love. Ultimately, Jason and the Argonauts are trapped on the Danube River by Aeetes army. The army is led by Medea's brother, Apsyrtus. Apsyrtus has come to bring Medea back to a vengeful King. This leads Jason and Medea to the death moment.

Jason must murder Medea's brother, Apsyrtus, to save Medea and himself. But this murder angers the gods. Jason and Medea must go through a ritualized process of atonement, before they can finally be free. Then they can marry.

There is simple structure here. I think you can see it.

A MORE COMPLEX PROTOTYPE

Let's look at another prototype . . . You have a Hero, she is not very heroic. She has a day job. She is raising two daughters alone. The husband has split. She has an inner conflict. Let's say her family has convinced her over the years that she has no self-worth. It is something that gnaws at her internally and will affect her decision-making. An unusual event occurs in the first few minutes. It could be a bad thing. It could be a good thing. Let's go with good. A girlfriend invites her to go on a singles cruise to find men. This is the inciting incident, the Adventure. The Hero elects to take on the Adventure. It becomes her goal.

The Hero meets a man(the Enemy). The Enemy has one goal: to throw up obstacles, to charm, to confuse, to fight, to keep the Hero from achieving her goal. The movie becomes a series of engagements, games, or battles between the Hero and various men. The engagements or battles progress in terms of costs to the Hero. The battles also create conflicts internally for the Hero. But our Hero has an innocence about her. It is a kind of blind innocence. She wants to trust. She wants to love. The first major battle costs the Hero a little. The next major battle costs the Hero a lot. One is personal to the Hero; maybe the next one affects her job and her finances. These are conflict situations. They are not just physical conflicts. The best conflicts thrust the Hero into a moment where the Hero must make one of two choices. If she acts toward her goal, she is betraying "family," or something old and dear. If she doesn't act, she loses. Somewhere around the middle of the movie, the Enemy completely devastates the Hero's world. Let's say the New Man dumps her. Or her best friend is hospitalized from domestic abuse. Or both.

The Hero keeps fighting. She is in trouble now. Let's say the new boyfriend has stolen all of her money. But, she keeps fighting. She keeps wanting to believe. Goodness will be rewarded. But there is another major battle to face. Let's say the ex-husband returns. This opens an old wound, the family wound. The old "tapes," the old way of thinking, show up in this scene. The Hero has been fighting valiantly the whole movie to get away from this sense of worthlessness. But it shows up here. She must give up her illusion of family, her illusion of love, whatever it is. She suffers.

However, a seed is planted in this moment of loss. A new tiny plant of sudden wisdom rises from the ground. There is a "secret" that has been hidden for the entire movie. The Hero looks squarely at the secret. She will proceed to the stronghold of her own personal Enemy, her Mother, her family. She will break the stronghold of family. She will bring reunion, even though she is the victim.

Now, our Hero can try love one more time. But, this is a smaller, quieter battle. It is more of a victory lap. Our Hero is already winning.

SUBURBAN DREAM PROTOTYPE

One of the best uses of the Enemy in current storytelling is an abstract Enemy. An invisible Enemy. A place, a repressive community, or family. Some of the most creative writing is coming out of the new American suburbia: high school movies. Everybody in the story shares the same goal. They have to get the grades, pass the SATs, gain admittance to a prestigious college. And somehow each character wants to over-come his feelings of inferiority and personal geekiness to gain acceptance within the group definition of "cool."

These are ensemble movies. Each of the Heroes faces the same Enemy. It is suburbia, a place, an ideal of American life; it is "The American Beauty." It is the crushing expectations of a sanitized suburbia and, especially, parents who are too self-involved to love. Each of our Heroes shares a similar inner conflict, too. Each Hero has a personal family wound that shames him or her.

There is one major structural demand for this kind of story. Each of the Heroes must find a cause, an opportunity, another person he can latch onto. This becomes his goal, his hope. The various Heroes may appear aggressive, maybe even self-destructive. And, they will be viewed as self-destructive by the collective power structure. The collective authority does not want to give away power.

One of our Heroes, let's call him Roy, is on a crash and burn. A series of crimes have been perpetrated in suburbia. The authorities suspect Roy, and want to finger him. But Roy is becoming more outrageous. His friends want to save Roy. His parents want to turn him in. But Roy doesn't want to be saved . . . Roy didn't commit the crimes. Roy knows a secret. This is why he is on a crash and burn.

There is one major insight you should gain from these prototypes. It is absolutely essential to good storytelling. I have come to recognize that it is present in every story. Every scene, all the engagements, the battles, the good news, the bad news, the friends the

Hero meets along the way . . . everything that you write should be leading your Hero directly to a moment of suffering. It is in this moment that the Hero faces her inner conflict.

TAMAR

I want to share an experience I had while channel surfing. I was flipping through some bad cable movies, the Discovery Channel, C-Span, and I landed in the middle of a religious program for young people. The audience was a good cross-section of Southern California kids, many of them wearing gangster attire, shaved heads, earrings, tattoos. They were sitting in bleachers listening to a youth minister talk about incest. He was telling them the experiences of several victims. The shame, the rage, and confusion that these people were feeling. It was pretty disturbing stuff. But I couldn't stop watching it. Then the minister started telling the classic story of King David's beautiful daughter, Tamar. Her half brother, Amnon, desired her. He was obsessed with his desire. He staged an illness and insisted that Tamar come to his house to make cakes for him. Tamar made cakes for Amnon, and then Amnon proceeded to rape her and throw her out of his house. Amnon now hated Tamar. His hatred for Tamar devastated Tamar, even more than the rape. Tamar became an outcast in Jerusalem, although her father was king. Tamar put ashes on her head and tore her robe of many colors. She had nowhere to go in this society as a rape victim. She lived out her days as a broken woman in the house of her brother, Absalom. I was watching this program. The story moved me. The faces of the kids in the audience were darkened and sad. I sensed that some of them have had first-hand experience with abuse. But, suddenly, the youth minister looked up at them and grinned. He said, "I have good news for you. Because of Jesus' death on the cross, you can get rid of the pain; you can be healed of these wounds. Come to me and I will give you rest."

Suddenly there was a lifting in the room! The kids jumped up and started cheering. Some of the gangster kids were giving each other high fives.

I was amazed at the simplicity of the storytelling. Yes, there is a built-in symbolism that all of these kids accept. There was a huge narrative jump cut between Tamar's Old Testament story and the New Testament symbol of the Cross. However, regardless of what your religious beliefs are, this storytelling worked. It worked on the kids in the audience. It worked on me. I suddenly thought, this is the purest example of storytelling: You have a beautiful Hero. You have an Enemy. The Hero experiences suffering and great betrayal. There is an act of sacrifice. There is redemption. Betrayal, suffering, sacrifice and redemption. This is story telling in its purest form.

THE SIMPLEST PROTOTYPE

This is a classic model that everybody in Hollywood uses. In Act 1, you chase your Hero up a tree. In Act 2, everybody throws rocks at him. In Act 3, the Hero climbs down from the tree.

CHAPTER 3

THE IDEA BEHIND YOUR STORY

We are sitting at your kitchen table. You and your partner are ready to plot. We still haven't completely defined what a story is, have we? We have established that there are certain prototype elements or sections that seem to work in building a story. But we still haven't gotten at the core of what a story is. What is missing? . . . The idea behind your story, what you are talking about.

Ultimately, there is a reason why you and your partner chose a story to tell. You love the story. It makes your friends laugh. It works at restaurants every time. There is something universal about the story. Maybe it is a story about a friend of yours who is married but eternally unhappy. He goes from job to job, but always says the wrong thing. He is brilliant but is reduced to selling pots and pans. Finally, he hatches a scheme to sell multi-level air filters. He is going to be the next Tony Robbins of air filters. Your story works on strangers. They don't even know him and they laugh at the guy.

But, here's the rub . . . behind the story of your Unhappy Pal is an idea. It is your idea. There is something in his adventure that strikes a chord in you. Perhaps it is something about how America treats losers, for example, that upsets you . . . or, there is something about his eternal optimism that gives you hope. In other words, behind your story, there is emotion.

Just as important, there is something in your Unhappy Pal that you believe that you see that he doesn't see. There is something in his confused psyche that you believe is blocking him from succeeding in life . . . There is something in his confusion that upsets you, or makes you sympathize, that you wish you could change in him. But, you are thankful for the very fact that he doesn't change, because then the storytelling would stop. You know inherently that his confusion is dramatic. However, this is a part of your idea, too. There is a personal philosophy behind your story. You believe that if your Unhappy Pal would come to terms with his wound, if he would get rid of this one way of doing things, then his life would be different.

At this point, you need to create a question. A lot of writing gurus label this "the premise." I like to think of it as "a question." Can our Unhappy Pal get through one weekend of important meetings without blowing it? There may be a deeper philosophical question that you are examining. Maybe your Unhappy Pal was doing very well at one time. But he had a bad car accident. It started a series of bad events. You show the car accident in the beginning. You jump cut to our Unhappy Pal in his present mode of self-destructiveness. So maybe the real question you are asking is a question of fate. Can our Unhappy Pal overcome a twist of fate?

This is your idea. Before you and your partner begin to construct a plotline, you need to define your idea, because this is a story. Ultimately, every movie is a mystery story. Whether it is a comedy, a romance, a drama, or an action film, it is still a mystery story.

Everything you do with your plot should drive your Hero and your audience to this moment of mystery. If your plot does this, you are telling a story. If you plot doesn't do this, you are not telling a story. A movie is really a treasure hunt. It is a treasure story movie. The plot should work as the map that leads us to the buried treasure. The treasure is revelations and secrets. Let me suggest something. Once we hit the cave of the buried treasure, all of the revelations do not come seeping out of the ground in the same scene. So relax with that knowledge. It is accomplished once in a while in a movie. But, in most movies, the revelations come out in several scenes. Usually the secrets of our Enemy come out in the big scene, and the Hero is brought face to face with his own inner conflict. It usually requires an additional scene for the Hero to get an additional revelation. Then, he can change.

You may be thinking: how can I accomplish this? We are going to discuss this scene or scenes in great detail later in the book. I am going to show you how a number of movies solve these scenes. This is still the best way to learn to do it. It is the way I have learned.

In the meantime, I am going to make a couple more suggestions. Let's return to our story of the Unhappy Pal. Part of your idea is your emotion that you feel beneath his predicament. I suggested, as an example, that you may be angry at the way American society treats losers. Well, then you and your partner need to create scenes along the way where the Enemies . . . his Boss, Fellow Employees, a Lady that he meets, his Wife . . . defeat our Unhappy Pal because he is a loser. You need to be slamming home "your truth" to him in scene after scene along the way—before he hits the cave of suffering and revelations. This makes the revelation scene a lot easier for you. You don't have to say as much. Your Unhappy Pal has been receiving lessons the entire movie.

Also you need to create friends who teach him. This device is pretty obvious. It is used in practically every movie. Think of yourself with your Unhappy Pal. How may times have you tried to talk to him? How many times have you tried to tell him that the way he is doing things is the wrong way? You need a friend as a mentor in your movie. Additionally, movies these days are utilizing friends in another powerful method of teaching. I refer to these friends as Secondary Heroes, or Sidebar Heroes. You give these friends the same inner conflict. They are facing similar Enemies. They are making the same mistakes. So, your Unhappy Pal can see a mirror of himself in their mistakes.

There is a third device that the best of the current movies use. I have already mentioned that we need to see the Hero's inner conflict in one quick graphic scene at the beginning of your story. Now bring your Hero face to face with his Enemy in the big battle scene. See if you can duplicate the initial inner conflict scene in this confrontation. This to me is the art in cinematic storytelling. You don't have to do it. But if you can do it, it works great. Think of it as returning to the scene of the crime.

BIBLICAL REFERENCE

Maybe some of you wonder why I reference literature from the Old Testament. Maybe you are thinking that I have some hidden agenda. The answer is no. The reason I examine these stories is that it is easy to see the moral debate within them. There is God's way and Man's way. There is the way of the spirit and the way of the flesh. A man is spirit and a man is flesh. In every situation, he is conflicted, he is torn. Studying these stories simply helps me to understand a man or woman facing an Enemy. Internally, he or she faces an even more difficult crisis, separating one argument from the other argument to determine what action to take. The more we, as writers, infuse every major confrontation in our stories with an excruciating internal debate, the closer we are to writing a great piece. We are living in a society in which traditional moral codes have begun to breakdown. No wonder it is difficult for us as writers to create emotional characters who struggle with inner debates.

There is second reason to reference these stories. The writing is very minimal and highly compressed. It is an easy way for me to study *progressions* in storytelling without a lot of reading time. For example, I like to study Shakespeare, to study his mastery of story progression. However, to read Shakespeare, most people require an Oxford translation. You need to examine the differences in the meaning of the language for Shakespeare's era to our own. It generally takes about three to four hours reading time. It is still worth it. And I do it.

I find building progressions in storytelling, building three major plot shifts that progress, the most difficult demand in screenwriting. Sometimes I feel mentally dry in this area. We can't just watch other movies and do riffs of their ideas. This is when I like to read some of the Old Testament stories to look for ideas. The economy of these stories allows me to see epic level progressions with a reading time that is only a matter of minutes.

Let me use the Biblical story of Joseph as a classic example of this. What is the inner conflict that lingers in Joseph? His brothers betrayed him. His brothers sold him into slavery and bondage. His brothers are his Enemies. They do not believe his dreams and visions. Joseph is prophetic and they hate him for it. What is the great, buried treasure scene? Joseph faces his brothers now as the Prince of Egypt. The brothers are now in *captivity* to Joseph. The brothers are at Joseph's mercy. The physical action of *captivity* is present in both scenes. The revelations begin to come out in a series of scenes. The greatest revelation for Joseph is that he must forgive.

BACK TO THE KITCHEN TABLE

You and your partner are back at the table. Scenes, crazy ideas, usually jump out at you in random fashion. This is great. This means the subconscious is opening up. So write these ideas or images down. Most writing teachers suggest that you write them down on individual note cards. If you ever take a writing class, the instructor will probably talk about this. Pick up one of the popular How-to Screenplay books at the mall, and the author will also suggest this method. In fact, most writers I know do this.

Eventually you begin to shuffle the deck. You begin to look at your scenes in various combinations.

This is also great. It forces you to move away from your conscious mind. The conscious mind wants to control the shape of your plot. Shuffling may give you a better shape.

However, this is where I tend to disagree with the enthusiasm for card shuffling. When I try to free form an idea, and I don't have at least a primitive picture of my major progressions, I tend to get nowhere. I can sit and keep adding note cards for weeks. I will end up with two stacks of note cards, and then three stacks of note cards.

This is exactly what happened to a friend and I about a year ago. We decided to tell a comic story about the dating scene in L.A. My friend is real big on the note card method. We started meeting at Hamburger Hamlet to work. We started jamming ideas and putting them down on note cards. Every week or so, I would try to construct a plot model from our note cards. My friend wasn't interested in this. He kept coming up with more ideas and note cards. He would say, "The writing books tell us to resist plot as long as possible." The end result was three months of creating note cards at the Hamburger Hamlet. We finally gave up. We never wrote the story.

What do I mean by progressions? I will spend an inordinate amount of time in this book on the subject. Progressions are the major shifts in your story. Sometimes these shifts occur as a result of a major event in your plot. Most people in Hollywood refer to these events as the plot-point scenes. But, sometimes a progression is not even a single event. It is simply a passage of time. Or it is a new test or obstacle the Hero faces.

For example, in a teenage love story, boy meets girl. There is a brief courtship. After a couple of comic obstacles, it becomes a relationship. This is a progression. In the middle of the movie, they break up. This is a progression. Then the young woman finds out she is pregnant. This is the next progression. I think you get the point. Again, we will discuss this in depth later in the book. The point I am trying to make is that it is better to have some picture of these progressions while you are writing the note cards. Don't make the mistake of my friend and me. Otherwise, you could be picking up a lot of checks at the Hamburger Hamlet.

WHEN TO WORK

I work best in the morning. My partner, Alex Lasker, and I made this discovery in our very first screenplay. We found that we needed to begin work everyday at noon. This allowed us to get up, do some chores, get a minor workout in (to get the blood flowing) and then we would meet. We discovered quickly that our minds worked at maximum with this ritual.

We also discovered that our best creative energy was expended after about four to four-and-a-half hours. Whenever we tried to write beyond this time allotment, we would begin making poor creative decisions. If we needed to add a second session, we would break for a few hours. We could pick up a second stretch after dinner. Our minds would refreshed, and we could work with clarity again for another three- to four-hour period.

I realize that many of you will have to write while carrying other jobs. It's a phenomenon that I have been aware of throughout my career. Don't despair. I have also been in situations like this. At those times, I still take advantage of the early hours. I write down the most creative ideas for a scene, including the key lines or events that come to me . . . in these early hours before I do other things. Your unconscious is most alive when you first awaken. You have been dreaming all night, sometimes these images stay with you. Write them down. But more importantly, your unconscious is still channeling for several hours after you wake, so your most creative impulses come at this time. This is always true for me. I write these impulses down. So even if I can't get to the actual writing until nighttime, I already have some great notes to work from.

If you are working with a partner, try to work at the same time everyday. Your conscious mind, your unconscious mind, and your energy level get used to this. If both of you have day jobs, pick a time in the early evening to meet. Make sure you have both eaten, and bring your notes. It is even better if you have taken a twenty-minute nap. Your mind will be rested and ready. The nap also puts out an S.O.S. to the unconscious mind.

A FINAL THOUGHT

We are going to be discussing a number of different ways that you can build your plot. We have just looked at prototypes. We will also look at my plot graph. We will discuss the simple Argument and Counter-Argument method. We will take a look at the

Good News/Bad News device; popular among younger comedy writers . . . You can use any of these approaches or a combination of them to tell your story. But, ultimately your story should lead your Hero to a moment of intense revelation. Knowing this should give you freedom. If you can define your philosophy specifically at the beginning, it will free you. You know that in one big moment, the revelations (of what you believe) will start coming out. You are telling a treasure story. We must find the buried treasure.

CHAPTER 4

METAPHORS

Miguel de Cervantes created one of the most enduring metaphors in all of modern art, even though *The Ingenious Gentleman Don Quixote de la Mancha* was first published in 1605. Painters have painted their impressions of this metaphor. Sketch artists have sketched it. The image of Don Quixote tumbling from his trusted horse, Rocinante, his lance caught in the blades of the windmill, defined Cervantes's tragicomic vision. This action defined the idea in such a profound way that it transcended plot, it transcended words, it transcended any need for discussion.

We understand it on a visceral level. We understand it on an emotional level. In other words, this brilliant piece of physical and visual action worked as metaphor. Cervantes was really talking to us about the impersonal destructiveness of modern industrialized society. It can kill heroism, child-like dreams, individualism, the artistic imagination. Don Quixote's embarrassment, his broken lance, resonates in all of us. This is just one episode in the hapless knight's long journey. However, it is spectacular. It is part of the zeitgeist.

My Webster's II Dictionary defines metaphor as "a figure of speech in which a term is transferred from the object it ordinarily designates to an object it may designate only by implicit comparison or analogy, as in the phrase the evening of life" . . . For our purposes as writers, I think we understand that it is a visual image,

33

a piece of action, a life-challenging moment that we are trying to create. When we are fortunate enough to discover this action, this life-challenging moment, we know it immediately. It should be cause for celebration.

Nathaniel Hawthorne, a romantic novelist from the nineteenth century, was a good practitioner of metaphor. Pick up a volume of his short stories, *Twice Told Tales,* for example. Hawthorne, like the English romantic poets, understood the power of sensory imagery taken from nature. He also understood dramatic situations, in which his Hero faced jeopardy of the soul. He understood that the combination of nature imagery and conflicts of the soul created great metaphors.

The short story, *Young Goodman Brown,* has haunted me ever since my first reading of it in college. The romantic Gothic imagery was ever present. The setting was chaste, repressed, puritanical Salem, infamous for its witch trials. Located at the edge of town was a dark, sinister forest, and even darker deeds. The weather was predictably damp, windy, and foreboding.

Young Goodman, who was a good man, ventured into the dark forest to participate in satanic rituals. It was his one night of sin. He discovered many of the pious townspeople indulging in the blasphemy as well. His discovery corrupted him.

The story still works as a prototype for American horror writing. The message of the metaphor is obvious. When a righteous man sees the evil in the hearts of others, he loses his own faith.

It is the opening of the story, however, that has always resonated with me. Faith, his beautiful young bride, symbolized innocence. She stood on the doorstep and begged Goodman not to venture forth on that darkest night of the year. She implored him to at least wait until morning's first light. In that moment, Goodman fought conflicting emotions. He felt genuine guilt. However, he acknowledged an uncontrollable dark urge. I have always felt that what Hawthorne was really talking about here was the irrational, lust impulses that lurk in the male psyche, even within the psyche of the most happily married man. It is like the modern husband who kisses his wife and children goodnight then sneaks off to his study to cruise the sordid world of cyberporn.

I can think of many movie images that worked as metaphors for me. Stanley Kubrick's *2001* is a great example. It remains a masterpiece. In the opening sequence, a family of apes was under attack from a rival clan. In desperation, they grabbed some animal bones and managed to fight off their attackers. The metaphor was simple and profound. Kubrick's vision of evolution was taking place right before our eyes. The apes had discovered the world's first weapon. The ape was becoming ape-man.

Kubrick expanded the metaphor immediately. After the surprising victory, one of the apes tossed the bone weapon into the air. The bone soared upwards and upwards, evolving into a modern spacecraft traveling into the far reaches of the heavens. Man was now fully evolved. His pursuit of tools and weapons allowed him mastery of the universe that would never end.

In *The Graduate,* Dustin Hoffman banged on the church windows like a hairy ape. He was trying to disrupt the wedding of Katherine Ross to a golden frat boy from Berkeley. Katherine Ross bolted from the altar and joined Hoffman in the foyer of the sanctuary. Hoffman added injury to insult by locking the raging wedding party inside the church. His actions became a metaphor for the baby boomers. It symbolized a whole generation's rebellion against parental expectations, materialism, the war in Vietnam, and settling down. It became a theme song of disaffection and alienation.

Early in the movie it was Ann Bancroft, as Mrs. Robinson, slipping her black stockings slowly off her legs. She manipulated Dustin Hoffman with the power of her sexuality. Somehow the scene became more than an act of seduction by an older woman. The boomers saw Dustin Hoffman as a metaphor of themselves. They were ready to cross a dangerous threshold into sexual freedom.

I also think back to the performance of German actor, Emil Jennings, in *The Blue Angel.* I first saw the movie in a film history class at UCLA. Subsequently, I've watched the movie many times. The image that will always stand out for me was Emil Jennings bouncing around the dance hall stage in clown face. Despite the makeup and the affected foolishness, you could see the absolute humiliation and horror in his eyes. Here was a reserved, university professor who had thrown away his career, his self-esteem, his life for Marlene Dietrich's jaded dance hall girl. Jennings was reduced to playing warm-up act to a room full of bored, horny men. This moment still remains for me, one of the most powerful metaphors of obsession that I have ever seen.

Sigourney Weaver made the cover of *Time* Magazine for the movie *Aliens.* Holding a giant gun in one arm and a little girl in her other arm, she was ready to meet the Mother of all Aliens. It was this image that helped propel the movie beyond the genre of action sci-fi and into the realm of movie classics. The movie became a metaphor for the strength of motherhood. Weaver became uber-mother.

Movie writing requires exaggeration. We all understand that. We are expected to find the big scenes, the intense emotions, the payoffs. I am simply challenging you to dig into your own experiences, and the experiences of your friends, for the surprising moment, the unexpected incident. You may be able to build that moment into a scene that is truthful and potentially symbolic.

Very few of us will face a moment like Sigourney Weaver did in *Aliens.* However, some of you might have experienced the seeds of this incident. Maybe you are a mother and you think you have just lost your child in a shopping mall. For a moment, you think that somebody has kidnapped your child. You saw two skinhead punks looking at your child in a toy store. It scares you. Now your child disappears. Suddenly, rage and power surge up within you. You start running to find the punks. You are ready to risk your own life. You would kill if you have to.

Why do some scenes work as metaphors and others do not? I am not sure anyone can answer the question. I am not sure great artists can answer that question. Perhaps, bottom line, metaphors originate out of

genius. This is strictly a hunch. We will discuss that
the Hero should be driven by an argument. He will
face the argument of the opposition. If the competing
arguments can approximate the primal arguments that
mankind has always faced, i.e., good and evil, flesh
and the spirit, science and nature, I believe it gives us a
better chance of finding this kind of scene . . . I also
think that is it important that the Hero should also be
facing spiritual danger, not just physical danger.

Many of us have been involved in a love
relationship that disintegrated like it did for Emil
Jennings in *The Blue Angel.* Maybe we didn't become
a clown in a dance hall. However, we have
experienced the seeds of self-denigrating behavior in
some form or another.

Recently, I was invited to put together a book of
short stories to be written by various Hollywood
screenwriters. The book is entitled *Hollywood Horror
Stories.* A writer pal, Dennis Woods, proposed a story
based on my experiences of losing a writing credit to a
famous movie star. The movie turned out to be
mediocre. However, as a young writer, this was my
first WGA arbitration defeat. I took it badly. I was
hired by the studio to develop the movie. It was my
screenplay that attracted the star. It was my screenplay
that was announced in the Hollywood Reporter as a
"Go" movie. Therefore, in the days leading up to the
arbitration, my representatives believed that I would be
awarded a split credit at the very worst. However, one
evening as I was driving down Sunset Boulevard, I
saw a giant billboard advertising the movie. To my
genuine horror, the actor was awarded sole writing
credit in giant letters. The WGA had yet to even

arbitrate the credit! But the studio had already banished me to Palookaville.

I had long since forgotten this incident until Dennis brought it up in a story meeting. He had never forgotten it. It resonated with him. Dennis took the incident and expanded it into a great hypothetical action involving my character and the billboard. When he presented his ideas, we all recognized a classic scene. We also realized it was a metaphor.

I agreed to contribute a story to the anthology as well. My story concerns a "Walter Mitty" type middle-aged husband who is locked in a loveless marriage. He decides to have an affair with a beautiful, young, trailer-park resident. I wanted to avoid the film noir clichés, in other words, shocking violence, or our Hero being set up for a murder, etc. Instead, I wanted to focus on the humor of opposites, and the possibilities for emotional obsession.

I immediately began jogging my memory for a payoff scene for my short story. I had the good fortune of meeting a young woman who grew up in the trailer-park culture. Over the years, we became friends. One evening, she invited me to accompany her on a dumpster run. I jumped at the chance. To my amazement, I discovered that there is a small community of lower class white folks that raid the dumpsters behind the Target stores, the Costco's, etc. They find furniture, clothes for the kids, CD players, you name it. I watched in wonder as this young woman climbed inside the dumpster and began to dig. What was even more endearing was that she had a great sense of humor about the whole thing. Apparently it was a family tradition. She learned about this from her mother and her aunt. The memory of this evening came to mind. I knew I had just found the seeds for my big scene.

CHAPTER 5

WHO IS YOUR HERO?

I have already suggested a prototype, a normal working guy or gal with a wound or inner conflict and some unfulfilled dreams. Why? Because this Hero is probably close to you, and most new writers base their first Hero on a version of themselves. This is not a bad thing. You know what you feel in most situations that you experience. You know when you feel jealous. You know what triggers your jealousy, and you know how you have acted it out. . . . In other words, you can be truthful to your Hero's emotion and his actions. Your Hero needs to ride a gamut of honest emotions in a story.

Using you as a model allows you to draw on real life episodes as a springboard idea for a scene. Occasionally, you get lucky and can use a real-life episode as the actual scene. But this is only on occasion. You exaggerate reality in movie storytelling.

We have begun to discuss that you have to be brutally honest about yourself. You must sit down with your partner. You must isolate a way of doing things that you understand will cause your Hero problems. In other words, you understand that your way of doing things causes you problems. And this way of doing things comes from faulty thinking. You must diagnose the root cause of this faulty thinking. You need to create an event for your Hero that shows us the root beginnings of this wound. This event is our armchair psychoanalysis. For example, if your Hero avoids violence at all costs, then we need to see a scene with the Hero where he is traumatized by violence, probably as a child.

Remember, your Hero is not just a person facing obstacles. Your Hero is a metaphor of your idea. Ultimately, your Hero must come to terms with your idea, and change.

USING SOMEONE YOU KNOW

I find that when I model a Hero on somebody I know, it gives me a kind of clinical objectivity and a strange freedom in running with the character. I tend to take more chances with a Hero based on a friend. Strangely enough, I generally see more comedy in the character. I tend to be merciless.

For example, I have a woman friend who is very attractive, intelligent, and controlling. She has dedicated herself to finding a husband *this year!* She is a very experienced television actress, and she knows how to act sweet, sexy, and California-girl submissive in the beginning of a relationship. However, her inner conflict, her almost fanatical need to control every situation, just like her mother needs to control every situation. It always surfaces on the very first date. Halfway through the evening, my friend cannot resist informing the gentleman of his psychological problems. To cap off the evening, my friend cannot stop herself from also informing the gentleman that she wants to be married by the end of the year. She asks her horrified date to declare his intentions.

It is easier for me to isolate a friend's faulty way of thinking and doing things. I tend to be a little more sensitive when I model the Hero on myself. I take myself too seriously . . .

Maybe your friend is a workaholic; your friend's conflict may be that he feels safe working, but unsafe with intimacy. Scrooge in Charles Dickens's *A Christmas Carol* is a classic example.

Your story dictates your Hero. If you are the Hero of your story, use you. Be thankful. Most writers do. The first screenplay my writing partner and I ever sold was a true comic adventure that happened while I was a student at UCLA.

Simply be a psychologist. Isolate the flaw in you. I am talking about an inner conflict that stops you from succeeding. It puts you into situations that you can look back on and say, "Why did I do that? That was so stupid."

CHANGE

There are two important keys to remember in creating your Hero. More so than any other character in your story, your Hero has to change because of the adventure. If he or she doesn't grow, you do not have a movie. You just have a plot. If your Hero is a workaholic, he learns to love . . .

If your Hero is a jilted big-city single Mom, like Sandra Bullock in *Hope Floats*, she learns to go home again to small town Texas. She must come to terms with her mother, find a job, and make it on her own. She learns to embrace simplicity, small ideas. She can then find a new man and let go of the cheating husband. She can change.

SUFFERING

The second key is suffering. During the Hero's adventure, the Hero has to suffer. Why? Don't ask me why. Ask the Greeks. Ask William Shakespeare. Ask the writers of the Bible. It just is. Aristotle's *Poetics* is what many of us read in college. Aristotle helped to define the aesthetics of drama. In its simplest terms, you create a Hero in high places. He must experience a fall, then he suffers. Audiences need to suffer with the Hero. Without suffering, your Hero will not arc. This is an absolute truth. So let me repeat it. Without suffering, your Hero will not arc. The bigger the suffering, at some point in the movie, the better the movie.

I don't mean suffering the whole movie. Audiences also want to laugh, they want to have fun, experience adventure and romance. I am talking about finding a key moment in the movie. The Hero has to fall on his face, be humiliated, taken advantage of, feel betrayed. It is in this moment that revelations can begin.

BIG HEROES

We need to mention another kind of Hero . . . the classic or epic Hero. Shakespeare loved to use Heroes who were Kings, or Queens, or the sons and daughters of royalty. In other words, he loved Heroes who came from high places. Of course, Aristotle and the Greeks were the mentors of Shakespeare, Marlowe, and all of the other great playwrights. A King or God-like Hero experienced a great fall from grace, primarily due to *hubris*, or pride . . .

Even with our working class guy or gal, we want them to experience a fall in the story . . . I believe Shakespeare, being the great dramatist that he was, also figured something else out here. The bigger the Hero, the higher his station in life, the bigger his fall. For Shakespeare, the big fall provided a bigger arc. If you sit around Hollywood story meetings at all, you listen to everybody knowingly talking about arc. "We've got to arc the character better" . . . start with a Hero who is a King. In our postmodern society, maybe you make him the President of a corporation. Halfway through your story, your Hero experiences a fall from grace. Borrow something from *King Lear.* His own family members vote him out in a stockholders meeting. He is reduced to president emeritus status. His children push him from house to house. He feels lost and betrayed. He slips into severe depression and later, emotional disorder. He is disenfranchised, lost on the cliffs, mentally deranged. This is a pretty good fall. This is a great arc. And, you need only one more transition.

A HERO IN CRISIS

Movie writers these days understand that we need to kick movie storytelling into Mach 2. The faster the start, the higher the stakes. The higher the torque, the less exposition, the better audiences like it. I feel it is necessary that we travel together through the normal steps of a Hero's adventure . . . A Hero starts in his normal world, there is an inciting incident, the Hero begins his adventure, etc. However, today's writers are looking for ways to put the pedal to the metal.

One of their main devices is to start the movie with the "Hero in Crisis." Nick Cage is fired by his agent in the first scene of *Leaving Las Vegas*. How many times have you seen movies begin with a Hero being fired from his job? Sandra Bullock is informed on national television that her husband is cheating on her in *Hope Floats.* In both of these movies, the Hero's crisis is also the inciting incident. But don't be confused by this. Some movies begin with a Hero in crisis and still give us an inciting incident. You are free to do it either way. It is your call. It is your story. But, just make sure to give your Hero a crisis.

Where do you find a crisis? Anywhere you look in everyday life. A parent dying is a big one. Your wife leaves you with a note on the refrigerator. You discover that a family member is stealing from you. In *The Sixth Sense,* Bruce Willis is shot in his own house by a former patient. This is the first scene of the movie. I would say that this is a pretty good crisis. It is also the inciting incident in this movie.

SENSORY HERO

This is the most important thing for you to remember. A character is revealed primarily by what he is doing, what he is trying to do and what he thinks about it. Your Hero has a goal . . .The stronger that goal is, the stronger your Hero is. You don't need a lot of funky character traits. At the risk of being pretentious, let me repeat it again. Your Hero is revealed by what he is doing, what he is trying to do, and what he thinks about it.

First of all, dialogue is not as important as you think. Progression of your story situations is what you, as a writer, must create. You let your characters react and work their way out of the various situations. How they react to these escalating situations, what they do, and what they think reveal the truthfulness of their character—not always what they may say. Your major movie stars tend to understand their personas. They are leading men and leading women for a reason. They act with their eyes. They are reactors more than actors. They are Heroes, and rely on what they are thinking in every scene. In other words, they rely on strong subtext.

I had the good fortune to work with Clint Eastwood on several movies. In *Sudden Impact,* he gave me a terrific acting role. My first day on the set, the production manager gave me the wrong information. He told me that we were doing a group scene. Instead, I discovered that we were shooting my "death" scene. Fortunately, I was trained as an actor. I had done my homework prior to location. It was a difficult scene in which Sondra Locke held a gun to me in my garage and I had to beg for my life. The monologue was nearly a page long, with several emotional transitions. I knew that, as an actor, I had to underplay it. It was shot entirely in close up. And I couldn't move. Clint Eastwood was directing the scene. We had no time to rehearse. We shot the first take. To my relief, Eastwood came up to me after the take and said, "That was great. You did that completely with your eyes."

Good acting is always in the eyes. What that means is your actor is working with subtext . . . what he is thinking. The best film actors prefer the non-verbal

47

moments. I had the good fortune to study with some of the great American acting teachers over the years. Basically, I was taught to answer certain questions coming into every scene.

What happened just before? If my character just participated in a robbery in the previous scene, residual emotions are going to spill into this scene. Even though my character may not say one thing about it.

Where am I? The place, the situation, of this scene is also going to affect my character physically, emotionally, sensorial. Start observing your own body language. Notice how different you behave when you are attending a formal function, as opposed to when you are having a barbecue.

What do I want in this moment? This, of course, connects with your Hero's ongoing inner monologue. What is your Hero's goal? What is he trying to do in your story, what is he trying to do in this scene?

Who is the other person? Your Hero is reacting to another character in the scene. What does your Hero privately think about this character? What does your Hero want from this character? What does the other character want from your Hero? Both of your characters should be bringing these thought processes into the scene, regardless of what the dialogue is. It should govern what they don't say as much as what they do say . . .

The final question is: What are the physical conditions? Is it hot? Is it cold? Is it a dirty, rat-infested alley? Is there a dead body sprawled on the alley floor several feet away? Are your two characters in a London tube station during a bomb raid, but are grabbing a moment of intimacy? The conditions will govern your characters' behavior as well.

You don't need to be pursuing a career as an actor to ask these questions. You can ask these questions as a writer when you are creating a scene. Most of these questions are non-verbal. They will help you create truthful behavior and dialogue for your Hero in a scene. It will reveal your Hero's character in a scene. As the late Lee Strasberg used to say in his classes, "intelligent actors make the best actors, because they think. Acting is thinking. Thinking brings on feelings. Not the other way around."

Don't let this impromptu acting lesson intimidate you. Do all writers sit down and ask all of these questions when they write a scene? Of course not. But I wanted to share with you a valuable lesson that I learned. From all my years of sensory training, I would always pick two sensory elements for my character in a scene—not one. If I were making the place in the scene positive for my character . . . I would make what happened just before a negative experience. This way I could be spontaneous in my performance. I would let the positive and the negative thoughts clash in my thinking while doing this scene. So from take to take, I would never be quite sure which thinking was taking over . . .

I think you can see how this can translate to your writing with your Hero. You know what his goal is. But, if you can be aware of his conflicting thought processes, you can take your Hero into a scene and let him struggle in subtext. Sometimes your Hero will struggle. Other times, your Hero will forge ahead in "blindness." But the magic is we as audience will

49

sense his internal struggle throughout. In *Braveheart,* Mel Gibson leads his rag-tag forces against a much superior English army at Sterling. The English send out an officer with a last offer of compromise. Mel Gibson's men are frightened. Many of them want to go home. Gibson charges blindly ahead. He wants to fight. Mel Gibson now looks at his men. He exhorts them, but we also see the conflict for Gibson in this scene. He knows that many of his men are going to die. We see this in his eyes.

A FINAL THOUGHT

Whoever you choose as your Hero, we must see evidence of his or her inner conflict early on. I devote an entire chapter to this, so I am only going to touch on it here. Think of it as a kind of "blindness" to the old wound, a "blindness" to the old way of thinking. Some movies nail it in an early scene. In *Meet the Parents,* you see Ben Stiller jeopardizing a patient in the hospital. Then you see him fumbling a marriage proposal to Teri Polo by being indirect and sneaky . . . Other movies don't give you that scene. They start in the middle of things. But, you still see it in the Hero's behavior. In *Pulp Fiction,* Samuel Jackson and John Travolta are driving toward a job. They are having a casual co-workers' discussion on the best hamburgers and the best bars in Amsterdam. They are actually hit men. They are about to murder some people. But they are blind to their line of work. They behave as if they are plumbers en route to fix a leaky toilet.

CHAPTER 6

WHO IS YOUR ENEMY?

The Enemy can be anybody. In a love story, the Enemy is your romantic "other half." European cinema loves bored housewife movies. You have a distant husband, a neglected housewife and a romantic rogue who moves into the village and opens a shop. The rogue is the Enemy. Understand, I am using these examples to stress that the Enemy isn't always bad. He just provides the opposition, the conflicts, the obstacles, the opposing argument for the Hero.

When I was a young actor, I was fortunate enough to work with the late Lee Marvin. He said, "Your Hero is only as good as his Enemy." I never forgot his words. I have heard variations throughout the years. Let me put it another way. Without the Enemy, we have no adventure. We have no battles. We have no plot structure. We have no movie. If there is a prize, our working girl can simply take it home with her. If it is a husband that she is praying for, she can walk up to the handsome rogue and say "you."

In technical terms, the Enemy is the person in your movie that engages your Hero in a series of complicated tests. I like to call them battles. Their purpose is to keep the Hero from achieving her goal. Winning the prize. Finding a new love. Getting married. Maintaining innocence. Solving the murder. Becoming a Navy Fly boy. Think of *An Officer and a Gentleman* . . . Richard Gere is our flawed Hero. He has one goal. He wants to survive the training to

51

become an officer, to fly planes. Louis Gossett Jr. is a classic Enemy, a hard ass, a slightly sadistic training sergeant. He doesn't like Richard Gere. Gossett's battles with Gere drive the movie. But *An Officer and a Gentleman* is also a romance. Debra Winger is the ambitious town girl. She becomes a second Enemy for Gere. Winger is emotionally complicated. She forces Gere to face himself. Gere is afraid of love. This provides the plot shifts in the movie.

Sometimes the Enemy can be an abstraction like Racism, Nazi Germany, prison life, or high school. In these movies, all the good guys in the story share a common opponent. This gives a richness and tension to everything that happens. But you still create one major Enemy that your Hero goes up against. If the abstract Enemy is high school, a bad teacher can be the one major Enemy.

BIG ENEMIES

As large, as expansive, as mysterious, as threatening as you can imagine . . . that is who or what you choose as the Enemy. The Enemy defines summer blockbusters. Big money is paid to young writers who can create big enemies. I don't know what it is about young audiences, the summer, and big enemies, but young people love the horror! Young imaginations crave the mystery of outer space, the threat of natural disasters . . . *Titanic, Aliens, Independence Day, Jurassic Park, Pearl Harbor, The Mummy* . . . Meteors crashing in on earth, the trenches of war, villains that usher in Armageddon. If you can think of a story using one of these mass threatening Enemies, you will sell your screenplay. Even if your writing is not that good.

Audiences also want people stories, love and romance, but they want them crafted on this big canvas. They want the magical unknown and the power. They want the Big Enemy. It is the shadowy menace looming on the horizon. It grows larger, but our main characters don't see it. The audience sees it. They see it in the buzz a year before the release. They see it in the trailers two months ahead. They see it in the Memorial Day lines around the block.

It is primal, this relationship between the audience and Big Enemies. It comes from the dark recesses of childhood nightmares and imaginations . . . the dark brooding monster. The dreams of falling through space, watching hundred-foot waves crashing into your house. It is the wonder that we all have. The secret worry and fascination we all share: what it would be like to know that we are about to die? If a meteor was crashing towards us, and we had ten minutes, what would we do? If we die, what happens then?

If you are trying for the Big Enemy, it has to seem fresh. The big game in Hollywood every year is to figure out "fresh." We began with the Jerry Bruckheimer big action, big star vehicles. There is only so much you can do with car crashes and explosions. We moved to outer space. We moved to mass destruction, Enemies from the past, knights and medieval butchering armies, the Titanic. Now we are recycling World War II again.

Dennis Tito, the multi-billionaire, bought his passage with Russian Cosmonauts into space. He paid a cool twenty million dollars. Now movie director

James Cameron is doing it. At the moment of this writing, Cameron is in Russia completing his cosmonaut training. Then he gets a ticket to ride on the next Soviet rocket. What is he doing? Cameron is looking for his next big movie Enemy. He openly admits it. His next screenplay is going to take place in outer space. He is looking for a fresh and exotic take on a fresh Enemy. He has offered the Soviets a percentage deal of his movie for the ride. That being said, if you can come up with a Big Enemy, congratulations. Fantastic.

Audiences loved *The Matrix* a year ago. Now two more *Matrix* sequels are being shot. To the brave new audience, this is a fresh new Enemy fighting life and death battles inside cyberspace. The fact that it is not truly fresh makes no difference. For those of us who are William Gibson fans, it is old hat. It has to be over a decade ago that some of my pals and I discovered Gibson. I read all of his novels two or three times. *Neuromancer, Mona Lisa Overdrive, Burning Chrome,* and so on. So the fact that cyber punk Heroes hacked into the Matrix in his novels, so what? *The Matrix* is fresh to this audience. It gives them a new Enemy. And they love it.

Of course, since the horrors of September 11, the "Attack on America" by Osama bin Laden and his terrorist network, Hollywood was doing a justifiable retreat from weapons of mass destruction . . . now they are back to movies of mass destruction, like *The Sum of All Fears.*

J. R. R. Tolkien's *The Lord of the Rings* trilogy offers us a nice alternative universe. Sauron, the dark Lord, is still the Big Enemy. He wanted the power of the ring to control the world. The darkness of Mordor is still a world of unspeakable evil. The landscape is safe for our post-terrorist audience because it is essentially epic fantasy. The world is essentially medieval, the weapons are swords and sorcery, not high-tech fire power. The Enemy is still big and horrific, but he is fantasy. The landscape is safely distant.

If you are going to find the Big Enemy, our discussion of the smaller Enemy still applies. The Hero still must share a relationship with the Big Enemy. Your main plot shift scenes should be encounters, twists, and shifts of power between your Hero and his main opponent.

FINDING THE PERFECT OPPONENT

You choose your Hero. You isolate his flaw. You determine his faulty way of thinking. You determine your Hero's goal. This is the Hero's "Argument." Choose an Enemy that has a opposite "Argument". . . or, as close to opposite as you can think of.

I want to make a really important point here about your approach to your Enemy. I say that you want to give the Enemy an opposite argument. I mean that in a philosophical sense. In most cases, the Hero and the Enemy want the same thing. They are fighting for the same prize, be it love or money. They just come at the prize from opposite points of view.

Let me try to offer an example. Let's say we have a well-intentioned Stanford professor who is doing ground-breaking research with marijuana, for medicinal purposes. The state government has just put a stop to this kind of research. There is a group of outlaw weed profiteers operating up in Humboldt County. Our professor travels up to Humboldt. He makes a deal with the growers that allows him to set up a research lab, hidden in the giant redwoods.

I think you can already envision where this story is going. Our professor has found hope. He can conduct research for the good of the world, even though he is working with some illegal traffickers. This is his argument, or goal. The prize is the marijuana plant. The professor's argument is essentially innocent, albeit naïve. The traffickers want the same prize. The marijuana plant. But they come at it with cynicism and an outlaw, get-rich-quick philosophy. So this is their argument. However, you can see that it is essentially two sides of the same argument. This is basically what I mean when I talk about opposite arguments. This is an important distinction, too. Because in your best storytelling, the Hero eventually gets beaten by the very thing he tries to embrace. We will talk about this some more later.

Think about it this way. Herman Melville's *Moby Dick* is one of the great novels of the last four hundred years. What was Ahab's strongest drive, his argument? He wanted to kill the whale. Who was the Enemy? The whale, although the whale was an innocent non-participant. The prize they were fighting over is life itself.

Let's return to my controlling television-actress Hero. She finally met her match. The man was a silky smooth, completely amoral player. He was six-foot-four, handsome, and rich. He would agree with everything she said, and then did whatever he wanted to do. He was tricky and seductive. She would talk about marriage and babies. He would agree, give her a new Rolex, then insist that the two of them watch the Playboy channel. This woman was a control freak, yet this man kept my friend constantly out of control. This is a good Enemy.

Look at your Hero. Figure out his one most obvious desire, the one thing that most drives him. Hugh Grant in *Notting Hill* is a good guy. He wants to find a good marriage partner who will love him. Tom Hanks in *Cast Away* wants to succeed as a FedEx boss, he wants to beat "Time". Now create your Enemy, a person or entity that is the best opposing argument you can think of if you are Tom Hanks and you are obsessed with beating time, what better Enemy than fate? Fate allows you to crash your plane, end up deserted on an island. Time stops. You can't even keep time . . . If you are Hugh Grant as Mr. Nice Guy, and you want a nice girl to love, what better Enemy than Julia Roberts, a spoiled American movie star? Besides the movie star issues, she is an actress. What is the nature of acting? Pretending. In every movie, she has a new lover. She gets in bed with another actor and pretends to be making love with him.

The Enemy is the Hero's teacher. A good Enemy, whether he is in a comedy, a love story, or a thriller senses the Hero's inner conflict or wound quickly. Sometimes he knows it before they even meet. As the Hero and Enemy spar and progress with each other he raises the issue to our Hero in dialogue. He disarms the Hero, and causes her to question her ability to solve problems. If possible, the Enemy wants to create a battle situation that duplicates the Hero's old injury.

The Enemy knows that if he can create a conflict situation where the Hero's old negative tapes can come into play, the Hero will fail. The Enemy also understands the Hero's goal. He is constantly trying to undermine that goal.

A good Enemy sets up conflict situations. Ultimately, your job as writer is to draw your Hero into a battle with his Enemy where the Hero can see his old wound repeated or duplicated. In the Biblical story of Joseph, the scene of the brothers' reunion with Joseph is a classic example. The brothers were required to give one brother over in bondage to Joseph. It brought back Joseph's old wound, his bondage at the hands of his brothers.

Small Enemies . . . Abstract Enemies . . .
MY FAVORITE MOVIES

My favorite movies these days are independent projects, art house fare, simple stories of ordinary people just trying to get by. The Enemy here is generally silent, invisible. The Enemy is an Abstraction. If we are watching a movie about teenagers hanging out at the 7-Eleven, the common Enemy they face is usually mind numbing suburbia or uncaring parents. *American Beauty* is really a study of the weight of the suburban ideal, the American dream . . . In movies like *Your Friends and Neighbors,* an argument can be made that the Enemy is really all of us. Our friends, our neighbors, even our spouses; we are all enemies to each other. We are all dying for sex. The unseen Enemy here is commitment phobia, lust, or maybe it is just collective narcissism.

I encourage you to come up with this kind of Enemy. If you can spot one of these "ghosts" affecting you and affecting a group of your friends, you are on your way to writing an extraordinary screenplay that is not controlled by plot. I repeat, it is *not* controlled by plot. You can soar with your characters. I am going to give you a couple of outline notes from a project that I am developing. It is titled *The Bridge.* See if you can identify the Enemy . . .

It is a stifling, hot, barren desert community. The big city is three hours away by car. To these people, it is light years away. An auto-part assembly plant once provided jobs. It is closed now. The only hope surrounds a new bridge that is under construction. The bridge would cross the river. The bridge could bring an economic boom. Life. Developers might build a mini-mall, a new Burger King, a J. C. Penney.

The Roche family is the only family that have means. They own the beautiful great house that sits on a rise above the hill. But the Roche family has fallen on hard times since the death of their father. So the Roches rent their family house out and live in the trailer park or in the small bungalow homes like the rest of the town.

Bobby Roche likes to hang down at the construction site. Bobby is trying to beat his drug demons. He seeks God's help and figures he will make sandwiches for the workers. In fact, a couple of the workers play music. And that is all Bobby wants to do, play music and write tunes. Anna, Bobby's wife, has other ideas. She is tired of working as a secretary in Melvin's real estate trailer. She wants Bobby to claim power of attorney, and stand up to his sisters, Margaret and Rita Lee. Anna wants control of the Roche family home. Margaret is beautiful, twenty-eight, and living out a hopeless, loveless marriage. Margaret does nothing all day but shop, pamper herself, and imagine her freedom. Rita Lee is twenty-one, seductive, and powerful with men. She works in a video store in the next town, and figures an older man passing through is her best hope. Rod is a manic depressive. He has just moved to this nowhere land to work at the tiny radio station. Rod fosters two hopes, the beautiful Roche sisters, he'll take either one . . .

HIDDEN METAPHOR

It always helps if you are using a metaphor in building your story. If your metaphor is the fairy tale of a cinder girl (Cinderella), for example, you know that you are going to create a social structure of people, including family members, who disregard your Hero. They will actually create situations to keep your Hero from realizing her dreams . . .

By using this metaphor underneath your story, you immediately have a guide as to how to develop your Enemies in this story. There are two important points to remember. First, you must define your Hero's argument, or her belief system, her goal. You want to build your Enemies with as opposite a belief system as possible, and opposite goals. Secondly, your Enemies need to defeat your Hero's efforts in as many ways as they can. Obviously, if you are going to use the Cinderella metaphor, you will create a Prince, in other words a terrific, potentially-liberating love interest.

You will also create a collection of jealous, manipulative office workers, or siblings, or fellow students who are threatened by your Hero's beauty, intelligence, and innocence. You will also have a working model for creating some of your great plot incidents. You know that your Enemies will be trying to keep your Hero from rising above her circumstances.

CHAPTER 7

INNER CONFLICT

I am going to try to approach this with care. To me this is probably the single most important element in storytelling. And yet, it is the most elusive. It is the most difficult to execute, so set a goal for yourself. Begin with understanding it. Set a second goal to try to take this understanding into a major battle or engagement scene.

We are about to analyze three major engagement scenes in the middle of your movie. Most writing books refer to these scenes as conflict situations. But, they don't completely explain what is meant by the term conflict situation. Yes, there are books in the marketplace listing examples of hundreds of conflict situations. You have probably seen them. Classic situations like, "Your Hero takes the wrong briefcase by mistake. He discovers a stash of drugs inside the briefcase." What most of us come away with is the surface event. How many times, in romantic comedies, have you witnessed this scene? Your working girl Hero has a new Man Friend. But, suddenly, his former wife shows up. The fact is, they never got divorced. This is a conflict situation. You recognize this scene, right? It creates a shift. However, the best writing provides an inner battle within the Hero in the same moment, in the same scene.

I have struggled with this writing idea my entire career. You have to constantly work at it. We are talking about inner conflict again. I am going to suggest an easier way to understand it. Give your Hero two opposite ways of thinking. One is the Hero's programming, her wound. Her inner conflict. It is what the Hero has been taught. The second way of thinking connects to the Adventure, the Hero's goal, what the Hero is trying to accomplish . . . the Hero's argument.

Sometimes it is as simple as this model. You have a Hero. He has found hope (his goal). He is fighting through every obstacle, defeat, and setback to hang onto his hope. He doesn't want to look back. If he looks back, he will slip backward into the sense of worthlessness and uselessness with which he grew up. He stumbles in one major moment. His new hope seems to betray him. Suddenly, those old worthless feelings return, they overwhelm hope.

Let's create a Hero who is a lady cop. She is new on the force. In a great battle scene, our Hero needs to take action. She needs to shoot her gun. The Enemy is standing there. He has just murdered someone in an alleyway. He has dropped his gun momentarily. Our Hero has a split second window of opportunity. Her goal is to stop him. She needs to shoot the gun. But, her old programming, her old way of thinking, floods over her. Our Hero grew up in a super strict Catholic family. The Ten Commandments and "Thou shalt not kill" was programmed into her. Let's lay it on thick. An older brother killed someone in a convenience store robbery when she was fifteen years old. It traumatized the entire family. Our Hero has spent her adult life trying to avoid violence.

So here is our Hero in the middle of this battle scene. Her goal in the movie is to become a great cop. This is her Argument. This is her new way of thinking.

She must shoot the gun . . . But our Hero doesn't shoot. The old way of thinking is too strong. The Enemy uses the split second. He grabs his gun. He shoots her friend for good measure. He gets away. Our Hero could have prevented it. This creates a big shift in the movie. This is the surface event. But look how an inner battle is fought as well. An inner conflict between right and wrong, the new and old ways of thinking.

FINDING THE OLD WAY OF THINKING

I am going to put six resource areas on the table:
- Family
- Religion
- Politics
- Class structure
- Science
- Personal injury

There are many more that you can come up with. In my opinion, some of our greatest stories involve a Hero fighting for his freedom or for justice . . . But the old programming keeps getting in the way. Lets take a quick look back at the story of Tamar. She was raped by a brother. What interests me about this story are the dramatic possibilities. I could see her having an anguished confrontation with her father, King David. She wanted justice, but her programming got in the way. This was a rigid society. When a woman was tainted, she was tainted. This was what her society believed. This was what her father, the King, believed. Tamar thought this was what God believed. She caved in. She didn't fight back in the scene.

Let's look at one of our suggested movies and examine inner conflict in action. In *The Sixth Sense*, Bruce Willis has an old way of thinking. If you prefer, in this movie, you can label it "one way" of thinking instead of "old way". Because it is a legitimate respected methodology. It comes from one of my six areas . . . Science. Bruce Willis is a trained child psychologist. He believes all areas of the human existence fall within the realm of natural or scientific explanations. He doesn't accept the paranormal. So what happens in the scene in the hospital? Haley Joel Osment tells Willis, "I see dead people." This is a new way of thinking. Two ways of thinking are clashing in this moment. A deeper nerve is being touched. Willis has a deeper inner conflict besides his job approach. He is dead. This is his "blindness" as a Hero. He is functioning as if he is alive. He is not ready to accept the notion that he can be dead, and still walking among the living.

I am going to suggest something. Aristotle defined the path of the Hero as a fall from high places, due to pride. Most movies these days don't give us Heroes in high places. American audiences love the "ordinary Joe." The Hero in low places. The underdog. People in high places are almost always the Enemy. So our Heroes' tragic flaw is generally not pride, or *hubris.* So, let's substitute "blindness" for pride as our Hero's flaw. And "blindness" is usually a faulty way of thinking.

Wendell Wellman

FIREFOX . . . TRIAL BY FIRE

Inner conflict is one of the most difficult and subtle elements to grasp. And I don't want it to confuse you, or discourage you from writing. I truly believe that if you and your writing partner launch into your screenplay, if you are using "You" as a model for your Hero . . . your subconscious will bleed it into your Hero's adventure naturally.

Remember, the team of Alex Lasker and Wendell Wellman began as naïve writers. We had no training as screenwriters. We wrote, and were paid to write, our first three screenplays, and we had very little, if any, grasp of how inner conflict worked. What we did have was a "bank" of good literature and good movies that we had read and watched. You have an even better bank to draw on. So we were being educated, as you are being educated. And, it does come out in your work.

But, I am going to give you one example from our first produced movie, Clint Eastwood's *Firefox*. Understand this, some writing teachers talk about the Hero's wound. Joseph Campbell calls it the "wound." I use the term wound a lot. Some teachers call it the Hero's flaw. Wound, flaw, inner conflict, we are really talking about the same thing. For the purposes of this book, I am calling it "inner conflict" because I want it to be an active element. I would like to see the conflict show up in a major battle scene. Getting to *Firefox,* Eastwood's Hero is a damaged Vietnam Vet pilot. He is suffering from "delayed stress syndrome" or post-traumatic stress disorder. We see this in one quick scene at the beginning of the movie. CIA operatives are searching for Eastwood. They are flying in a military chopper. Eastwood is taking a jog . . . the sound of the rotors freaks Eastwood. It brings back all the horrors of the war. It is a thirty-second flashback. Gunfire, napalm, burning villages. Eastwood is an Air Force pilot. He is running down a road. He sees an innocent Vietnamese girl. She is crying. She is lost. Napalm burns her to death. One quick scene.

Firefox was a book written by Craig Thomas. My partner and I were given the task of adapting the book to the screen. In our screenplay, we allowed the flashbacks, the delayed stress, to overwhelm Eastwood several times in big, stressful situations in the movie.

Here is the irony. At the time, we understood it was a "wound," but not as an "inner conflict". Recently, I was asked to do an interview on a cable television show. They wanted a clip from the movie. So I looked at *Firefox* again. I hadn't seen the movie in ten years. Suddenly, I recognized something in this little flashback scene. It is the burning of the little girl. She is an innocent victim of the war that Eastwood is fighting. That is the key. He feels guilty about it . . . This is what Lasker and I didn't recognize fully during the writing: his Hero's guilt. It isn't just war trauma. This is his inner conflict, his guilt, not just his fear of flying.

Then I looked at Eastwood's first big "battle" in the movie. He meets his Russian operatives by a river's edge in Moscow. They murder a man right in front of him. They beat him to death, then hand Eastwood the man's passport and credentials. Eastwood would now operate in this man's identity to complete the mission. Eastwood is horrified. At the subway station, Eastwood's delayed stress overwhelms him again. Great scene.

What is Eastwood's inner conflict? Another innocent victim has died, while Eastwood "serves the cause." This new scene duplicates the old scene in Eastwood's past. It brings up the same wound of guilt. The new scene duplicates the death of an innocent. Eastwood has a new goal. He must steal a Russian plane. But it clashes big time with his other way of thinking in this scene. His guilt and horror. He wants no more violence to innocents.

Alex Lasker and I adapted the book. Craig Thomas invented the scenes, so give Craig Thomas the credit. It is only now, in looking at the movie after ten years, that I see how great the scene was at the river's edge.

WHAT SHOULD YOU DO?

Create some simple quick scene in the beginning of your movie. Let it show your Hero's private wound, his inner conflict. Then try to find a moment in one of your battle scenes where he can face this inner conflict again.

THE HEROIC INNER CONFLICT

It is your option to determine which way of thinking you support in your story. You are the artist, what you believe is your idea. This is what you want your Hero to learn. Let's circle back to our pseudo adventure of the Unhappy Pal. I suggest that he suffers from a deep inner wound. This results in our Unhappy Pal always doing the wrong thing. There are some old tapes playing here and you, the writer, have to define what these old tapes are. Naturally, the old tapes clash with his new way of thinking. He is going to be the next Tony Robbins of air filters. Most movies use the old way of thinking as the hindrance to the Hero. For example, in *Meet the Parents,* Ben Stiller's old tapes result in Stiller constantly lying. But, you don't have to vilify the old way.

In some of our greatest stories, the old way of thinking ultimately proves to be right. The new way of thinking isn't always right. Sometimes the inner conflict is ultimately the right answer. But the old way of thinking still clashes with a new way of thinking. It causes great suffering for the Hero.

Look at the story of Moses from the book of Exodus. He grew up as the adopted son of the Pharaoh's daughter. He grew up with all the power, the privileges, and the education of Egyptian royalty. The Pharaoh's own son was Moses' best friend, his brother. This was his new way of thinking. The Jewish people were in bondage, as worker slaves. Moses had little to do with them. He had little identification with them. However Moses was a Jew, even though he wasn't raised Jewish. He was raised as an Egyptian with their religious training, their ways. Unbeknownst to Moses, he was God's anointed. This was Moses' other way of thinking. But as a young man, Moses was blind to it. Here is blindness again; the substitute flaw for pride. I am certain that as Moses grew up, he had many interactions with the Jewish people. These interactions probably disturbed him, made him feel guilty, brought up feelings of loyalty and questions about his relationship to Almighty God that were in direct conflict with his Egyptian Gods. The old thinking of his ancestors was flooding in on Moses. This was his "Calling." If you talk to people who have experienced this, they will tell you that it is very disturbing, "The Calling."

Now, look at the first big battle scene in the story of Moses. Moses didn't understand that the Egyptians were his Enemy yet. Moses thought they are his friends. But Moses witnessed an Egyptian beating a Jewish slave. It was a big plot point one scene. A great scene. Suddenly, it was not just an event scene. Moses experienced a tremendous clash between his new way of thinking, he was an Egyptian, and his old way of thinking, he was a Jew. Moses' old way of thinking overwhelmed him in this moment. He murdered the Egyptian guard and buried him. Why is it a great scene? Because it is both an outer battle, with an Enemy clearly defined, and an inner battle within Moses. It shifted the direction of the story. Moses was now an outlaw. He had to run. He had to live in exile.

HERO IN EXILE

The story of Moses is interesting to me for another reason. This is a theme that is often repeated in some of the great Hero literature throughout the ages. Moses lived in exile. He was a Prince of Egypt and now he was living with some lowly sheepherders in the desert. He was humbled and he lived there for many years. Imagine the pain, and the mental suffering he experienced . . . because of choosing one way of thinking. "I sacrificed my royalty, everything, for my people. And this is how you reward me, God?"

Exile and suffering is an incredible section in the great Heroic story. The Hero didn't realize that this was part of the shaping of his Heroism. He was being trained, hardened. He didn't realize that soon he would return to the motherland as a great warrior. He would deliver a nation.

Here is the additional "hook" for me. Moses could have taken his wife and his child and left the desert. He could have started a new life. But he didn't. He waited on God. Even though the years passed and there seemed to be no answer. He kept waiting. This is the Hero's way. He endures suffering for a way of thinking. He never loses faith.

Joan of Arc died for her belief system. Mel Gibson's William Wallace in *Braveheart* died for his belief system. Russell Crowe's *Gladiator,* died for his belief system. Epic Hero storytelling wins Academy Awards.

FOCUS

Neil Slaven directed a beautiful small movie, *Focus.* Kendrew Lascelles adapted the screenplay, based on an Arthur Miller novel. The movie explores anti-Semitism in a Brooklyn neighborhood during World War II. The movie is slow going and meticulous. It is a textbook for demonstrating the clash of two ways of thinking. In this case, our Hero is William Macy.

Simply put, David Paymer is a Jew who runs a newsstand on the corner of the block. The crusaders, a collection of racist thugs, want his "kind" out of the neighborhood . . . William Macy marries Laura Dern.

71

Both Macy and Dern are trying desperately to fit in. Laura Dern is hiding her ethnic heritage. She is in denial. Macy simply "looks", from the thug's point of view, like he could be a Jew. Our protagonist newlyweds are driven by a goal. They want to be accepted in the neighborhood. They want to disassociate themselves from the victims, from people like Paymer.

. What is beautiful about this movie is that whenever David Paymer stands alone in the street, he functions as a gnawing metaphor for Macy. Macy is in denial of his own sense of justice. At the beginning of this story, Macy observes a woman being brutally raped. He does nothing about it. Macy sees Paymer suffer indignities. He does nothing about it. At various points in the story, Paymer walks out into the middle of the street. He looks longingly at Macy. He is a moral challenge to Macy. It is simple, poetic, done with few words. We as an audience get it. Macy is torn between two arguments.

A number of movies will use this structure. Each way of thinking is represented by a character or group of characters. It builds the structure this way. David Paymer becomes the Good Enemy. The neighborhood becomes the Bad Enemy. Macy is torn between the two.

CHAPTER 8

THE HERO'S ARGUMENT

THE IDEA ... THE ARGUMENT ... WHAT?

All screenwriting books attack the subject. Some call it "the sustaining idea," others call it the "theme," still others refer to it as your "premise," and some even try to make a distinction between "theme" and "premise." I would read these chapters and I would get it on an intellectual level since I have a literature degree from UCLA, but I would not get it on a writing level. How do I write a theme? In movie writing, which demands so much structure, so many character quirks and plot twists, how can I possibly write a theme? Naturally, none of the screenwriting books would answer this. If they attempt to answer it at all, it would be along the lines of: "this is where your talent comes into play," or "know what you are trying to say." Thanks a lot, guys!

A few years ago, I read an interview with Oliver Stone. He was a little over the top in the interview. But basically he talked about writing, and said something that I really responded to. The paraphrased version is, "I cannot write unless I am angry about something."

I thought, "Yes, that's it!" That is basically my argument. Whatever story I choose to tell, I have a Hero who faces an adventure. But, behind the story, there is an idea, a question, an issue or a personal experience that I, as a person, am bothered about. This is my argument. The author's argument. How do I solve this issue? The whole story should function as my effort to examine what bothers me.

You may be annoyed right now. You are probably asking, "Why do I need an Argument?" You are ready to plot. My answer is, you need an argument; otherwise you are just relying on plot. Your argument shapes your plot.

Let me give it to you in a simple package. This package works for me. About a year ago, I was having a discussion with a friend of mine, who is one of the top story analysts at Disney. We were trying to get a handle on all of the new multi-character, multi-structure (ensemble-style) movies. We began discussing the Hero as one side of the argument. The Enemy is, of course, the opposite side of the argument. Suddenly, a light bulb went off and I felt a sense of relief. Here is structure. In other words, when all else fails, we can return to the story as an argument.

My Disney friend took it one step further. He said, "When I evaluate material at Disney, I always think of it this way . . . The first act is the Hero's argument. The second act is all of the arguments against it. And the third act is a kind of a low point of suffering . . . and a final resolution of everything."[1]

Let's stop right here for a second, people. Read my Disney story analyst's words again.

Act 1 = Hero's argument
Act 2 = all arguments against the Hero

---

[1] Peter Flood, Story Analyst, Disney.

Act 2 = suffering and the resolution of everything.

Here is structure for you in its most elegant, simplified form. If my prototype or plot graph model doesn't work for you, use this. You can plot from these three simple steps.

My Disney friend and I continued the discussion. I said, "let's add one more brick to the wall. In the low point of suffering, the Hero unravels a secret or insight for living. Then we can think of the third act as the author's argument". We both got excited again. In other words, what the Hero discovers that allows him to overcome his adversity, this is essentially your argument as a writer.

Let us go back for a moment to the Biblical story of Tamar, the daughter of King David. I began thinking about developing this story because it made me angry. This is my argument as a writer. I started studying the world at that time. I began to understand that the Enemy in this story was not the brother, Amnon. It was the social system. If I do choose to develop this story, I would have to come up with some solution for Tamar, some insight that would allow her to find freedom. This would be my argument as writer. This would be Act 3.

THE HERO'S ARGUMENT . . .
THE SIMPLE PLOT

Now let's take a quick look at my Disney friend's formula for a simple plot. The Hero's argument and "all the arguments against him." Don't get confused here. We have just been discussing your argument as the writer. What is the reason you are telling the story? What are you trying to say?

Your argument as writer is different from your Hero's argument. It is different from the Enemy's argument. Their arguments are naïve. They lack your insight. They lack your solution. Remember that the Hero needs an inner conflict. He needs a blindness to his flaw. The Hero will see clearly only in the end. In simple terms, the Hero's argument is his goal. It is what he is trying to accomplish without total understanding.

So, let's look at *Meet the Parents*. This is a classic illustration of Hero's Argument . . . and opposing (Enemy's) argument . . . What is Ben Stiller's argument as the Hero? I don't know the screenwriter. I have never spoken to him. But, after watching the movie, this is what I think the Hero's argument is . . . "I am a modern, urban, neurotic male. I am free to marry my WASP poster girl princess without conforming to her parent's expectations. I am a little geeky and I have a habit of being a little sneaky. So what? This shouldn't matter, right?" Wrong.

Look at the simple plot structure. From the beginning of the movie, Ben Stiller is pushing his argument forward. Even his attempted marriage proposal to Teri Polo is sneaky. He stages it with her students. They are supposed to be holding up "Will You Marry Me" cards behind her back in a store window. Teri Polo gets a call from her sister. Her sister's boyfriend wants the sister's hand in marriage. But he must get Teri Polo's father's permission first. Stiller wants to know why he needs the father's permission. HERE IT IS: Ben Stiller's argument is naïve. He thinks he can dive into an upper class society without paying attention to its rules and regulations.

The entire plot structure results from Stiller pushing his argument. Robert DeNiro and the family are knocking his argument down with opposing arguments, scene after scene. Stiller sneaks into Teri Polo's room to sleep with her. Wrong! DeNiro and Blythe Danner tell him they have a bed made up for him downstairs. Stiller sneaks into DeNiro's private office and snoops around. Wrong! DeNiro gives him a lie detector test. Stiller decides to discuss marijuana as the true meaning of "Puff, the Magic Dragon". Wrong! Stiller sneaks a cigarette on the roof of the family home. Wrong! This time, nature provides the opposing argument. It starts a fire.

You see how simple this is? This is an elegant, simple way to build a plot. It is not too far off from another plot principle we will discuss: Good News/Bad News. The Good News here is Ben Stiller's resistant optimism and Teri Polo's love for him. The Bad News is the opposing arguments of the family.

How would I describe all the arguments against him? DeNiro is the voice of these arguments. I think his message is clear. "We are a family. We have a way of doing things. If you want to marry our daughter, we want you to be a strong Man's Man. We want you to be a good provider. We don't want a drug user, a neurotic, and we don't tolerate sneakiness."

What is the author's argument here? Again, I am only going by what I see on film. My guess is that the author is probably a trifle angry at this kind of snobbish, rigid social set. They have a way of making outsiders feel pretty foolish. I had first hand experience of this. While in college, I tried to date an ultra WASP UCLA princess from the Palisades. I was invited to a dinner at her family mansion once, and I was made to feel like a complete idiot. The family had a rigid set of expectations for young men that included upper class family background, UCLA sports accomplishments, and money-earning capacity. I had none of the above. My guess is the author had a similar experience.

But the author is still fair. He recognizes that Stiller's sneaky behavior is also a big problem. In the end, Stiller learns that he needs to be honest. DeNiro learns a lesson, too. In the climatic scene, DeNiro and Stiller get "real" with each other at the airport. They negotiate. They get honest. I think this is the author's argument. People from different social systems can connect. But it starts with total honesty. Ultimately, it is really simple. When I say that you need an argument to tell your story. I am not talking about some deep philosophical or psychological treatise. It can be simple. It should be simple. With just a little truth.

THE PREMISE

So that we don't get confused, let's also try to define premise. The argument drives your Hero. It is what he believes, and it is his goal. The Enemy, or Enemies, come at him with an opposing argument. It is what the Enemy believes, it is his goal. So what is your premise, then? Basically it is the point of your movie. It is what the critics love to talk about in reviews. "The movie is a meditation on man's fate and destiny, and the power of love" and blah, blah, blah. You've seen the reviews.

All of this can still be confusing. The way that it works for me is to reduce my movie to a simple question. If the move is about fate, my question would probably be something like . . . Can a man recover from an accident that takes away everything? Or I might put it another way. Can my Hero change his destiny? In the movie *Notting Hill*, what is the premise? Can Hugh Grant overcome money and celebrity differences to find love and acceptance?

So, how should you deal with premise in your story? The question that you come up with is for you to think about privately. Ultimately, it is your idea. It is your point. But in terms of writing your script, it is easier to work with your Hero's argument. Remember that the argument drives the plot. If your movie is about fate, for example, your Hero believes he can recover from an accident. This is what drives him. The Enemy will try to answer him with the opposite thinking. He will pile defeat after defeat on your Hero. This is what you are trying to do. This how you design your story in the simplest of terms.

WHAT ARE SOME OF THE ARGUMENTS?

Let's play the quiz game. Think of movies with an argument. How about the "Good Man" argument? Your Hero is decent, moral, hardworking. His argument is - that if you work hard, do the right things, life should ultimately reward you. The Quiz Answer? Frederick March's returning war hero in *Best Years of Our Lives*. Tom Hanks's hard working, church-going

FedEx man in *Cast Away.* I guarantee you that screenwriter William Broyles Jr., Robert Zemeckis, and Tom Hanks understand this argument. In *Cast Away,* Tom Hanks and his wife even make jokes about *Best Years of Our Lives.*

What about Tom Cruise's "good doctor" and loving husband in *Eyes Wide Shut?* What about Tom Hanks in *Forrest Gump?* What about practically any movie that Denzel Washington stars in? What about Mel Gibson in *Braveheart* and *The Patriot?* What about Russell Crowe in *Gladiator?* Is there any coincidence as to why Tom Hanks, Mel Gibson, Russell Crowe, and Denzel Washington are four of our biggest stars?

How about the "Rob the Bank" Argument? In other words, the Heroes are likeable losers. They have suffered some big setbacks, some bitter disappointments. "We can break the laws of God and Man, just this one time and not suffer the consequences." Let's play the quiz game again. Do we even need to play this one? How about George Clooney, Mark Wahlberg and their Persian Gulf War buddies in *Three Kings?* What about John Travolta, Samuel Jackson and Bruce Willis in *Pulp Fiction?* Add to this the ad infinitum list of movies that are spinoffs of *Pulp Fiction?* My story analyst friend at Disney calls them "outlaw movies." He also says, "Who cares?" The last couple of years have brought us John Travolta and Lisa Kudrow in *Lucky Numbers.* Sean Connery and Catherine Zeta-Jones in *Entrapment.* These are just lighter versions of this argument.

How about Man versus Nature? Nature versus Man? Take a look at *The Perfect Storm.* Take a look at *Titanic.*

Now we enter the turf of science fiction. Look at a seminal classic like Stanley Kubrick's *2001.* Cut forward twenty-five years to good modern sci-fi like *Alien, Aliens 2,* or mediocre sci-fi like *Red Planet.* They are all begging the same question, aren't they? How far can man test the limits of Nature with man's science and technology? The Hero's argument is "If I can build it, if I can conceive it, I have the right to conquer it." The opposing argument is pretty obvious isn't it? "You play around with the laws of Nature, you try to be God, you are going to pay." Nature, the Universe, God's laws, these can be powerful Enemies. The great sci-fi writers, Arthur Clarke, Ray Bradbury, Robert Heinlein, Isaac Asimov, William Gibson, you name them, have always been obsessed with these themes.

CHAPTER 9

CREATING CHARACTERS . . . AND FRIENDS

Let me give you a few tips that I use. Whenever I need a character for a particular section of my story, let's say the Hero's friend, then I automatically go to my bank of personal friends and acquaintances. I trust my unconscious that one friend will jump out at me. I role model my character on that one person. That friend should have big opposites to my Hero. If my Hero is a quiet brooder, the friend is a talkaholic. If my Hero is on the hunt for love, my friend will be the suit-and-tie Married Man with two kids living in the Valley. Why? Because I can now have a funny dialogue between the two characters. The dialogue can touch on the Hero's goal, maybe his inner conflict. It is only a couple of lines in one scene, a couple of lines in another scene. You don't want to be preachy. But it allows you as the writer to externalize choices and the Hero's inner conflict for the audience very simply, very subtly, within a scene where both characters are trying to accomplish something else. This is the traditional method of developing other characters in a movie.

Multiple-character movies have really taken the use of friends to whole other level. There may be one identifiable lead character, but all of the major players go through complete story arcs. Essentially, all of the major characters are Heroes. The trick in this kind of writing is to create one common Enemy for everybody. The Enemy is usually an Abstract one, love for example. Each Hero is looking for love. Each potential love partner is the hope.

Now we watch all of our Heroes go through many misadventures with the various love partners. What is important to note is that this is essentially a new, better kind of mentorship. It is a great improvement in writing technology. It takes us a long way from the old cliché sidekick, or pal. Why? Because we are seeing "the teaching" through other characters' experiences, as opposed to advice. Experience is the best teacher.

We are going to examine multiple-Hero story-telling a lot in this book. But first, we need to look at the more traditional use of friends.

In *The Thomas Crown Affair,* Rene Russo is operating from her inner conflict in almost every scene. She is pursuing art thief, Pierce Brosnan. But she is in denial. Russo is falling in love with Brosnan. So who is the friend? Denis Leary's cop. Rene Russo is glamorous, a jet-setter, she has a house in Europe, a flat in Manhattan. She wears designer clothes.

Let's look at Leary's cop. He is scruffy, no frills, no relationship, his wife left him for a urologist. He wants to proceed by the rules of the investigation. Russo is constantly breaking all the rules. Big opposites, right?

Now lets look at a couple of their dialogue exchanges. Remember my point, Russo and Leary are working together, they are trying to accomplish a shared goal. So the scenes together are essentially investigative - try this tactic, try that tactic. So you slip in your friendly observations and "teaching" in bits and pieces.

Russo is crossing the line in her investigation and Denis Leary knows it. After an evening of dancing and sex with Brosnan, Russo shows up at the police station. Leary is staring at a photo of Russo's see-through dress. Leary's opening line is "Nice dress!" One line. But the subtext is "this is not just about insurance investigation. You want this guy." In another scene at Leary's office, Russo shows up after two days in the Bahamas. Her face reflects her feeling of compromise without saying a word. But Leary is on to her. Leary asks Russo (paraphrased), "Do you know what you are doing?" Russo snaps back, "I know exactly what I am doing. He likes me, and I can keep him close to me." But Leary nails her with his next line. He says (paraphrased), "What does that make you?" He hits Russo right smack in the core of her inner conflict.

Again, this is a traditional method of mentorship in screenwriting. There is a newer, more powerful approach to the development of secondary characters that we will look at toward the end of this chapter. But this is still an effective approach. There are three important principles that you should recognize:

1. Your Hero needs a friend. The best kind of friend is a big opposite. This creates built-in energy and humor to your scenes without you even trying. Humor carries movies these days. Audiences want to laugh.

2. Your Hero and his Friend should have a common goal, something they are doing together. This is very important. This gives your scenes with your characters more drive. You know what I am talking about . . . Your Hero and his Friend are trying to deactivate a bomb on a timer.

FRIEND
"Alright, we're doin' it, I'm taking a deep breath here. I am cutting the blue wire."

HERO
"No, the blue wire is positive. You cut the red wire."

FRIEND
"Man, I know which wire it is! Will you just shut-up so I can think!?"

But somewhere in the midst of this high-energy scene, the friend slips in the jab regarding the Hero and his Enemy.

FRIEND
"I mean, ya know, you go out and boff this chick and you think she isn't going to turn you over?"

HERO
"Stay out of my business."

FRIEND
"No, this is my business. It is our business. She probably has a wire in your apartment right friggin' now!"

Then they resume working on the bomb and diffuse it. Like I said, a couple of lines in one scene and a couple of lines in another scene.

3. By allowing the friend to throw in the occasional jab, you help the audience to understand the choices

your Hero is facing, and sometimes the inner conflict of your Hero as well. Your Hero rarely, if ever, talks about it. The Hero is only vaguely aware of his confused, old way of thinking. This technique allows the friend to verbalize for the audience the next big decision your Hero must make. And your Hero is usually making bad decisions.

So, let's return to my suggestion of role modeling a character on someone you know. Do you have to do this? No, of course not. If you use these principles, you are already way ahead of the game. Using someone I know helps me. It gives me built-in behavioral quirks without working on it.

Let me give you a quick example. I have a friend who used to be a dancer. She is now a lovely, intelligent divorced mother with a child. She is a high-energy, big talker kind of person, and she has this quirk. In the middle of a conversation, she will suddenly start doing some dance stretches, and sometimes she will execute a high kick. It's quirky, it's funny, I love it. But, I also know her well. I know her pain, I know her dreams, I know what makes her tick. I have already written one role for her. And she played the part. It was some of the easiest writing I have ever done. It was a stage production and her character stole the show. In her first entrance, she swirled onto the stage in a big fox fur with spiked heels. She tripped on her entrance, but talked in good humor about her husband who was cheating on her. She was a life force. She was undaunted. She was calling her nanny on the cell phone. The audience started laughing. They loved her, they recognized her. They kept laughing at everything she did. I allowed her to collaborate with me even during the rehearsal process. Sometimes I would call her up and say, "Here's the situation, give me a line your character would say here!" She would give me a line instantly. Her line would be perfect. Dead on. Better than any line I could have written.

Listen, one of the things that amazes me about writing technology in Hollywood is the constant focus on character development. There are seminars and classes going on every night of the week. Most of them focus on creating big, outrageous characters. "Push the envelope with your characters." "Ten techniques for your characters that are guaranteed to make studio executives sit up and take notice." I am curious sometimes, and maybe I ought to take some of these classes. But, the bottom line is I don't have time. I am usually writing.

I understand that Quentin Tarantino was a big wake up call for young writers. You see it in movie after movie. Big, crazy characters with drug problems, sex problems, and, most of all, a capacity for nonstop verbal riffs. A lot of these young writers are brilliant at it, they are media savvy and media obsessed, and they know how to let their characters riff on American pop culture. It's funny. I also do it on occasion . . . but, ultimately, you need your characters to speak the truth. In other words, underneath the mask, the audience needs to recognize these characters, to see something in the character that is them. To quote Bill Clinton, "I feel your pain." Somehow using real friends as a role model helps you to get to that truth. It is not the only way. It is one way that works.

PERSONAL OBSTACLES

One of the best ways to spin your character is to give him or her a personal obstacle. Traditionally, these obstacles were usually physical. Blindness, a speech impediment, a secret illness, epilepsy, and the like. You can still do this and if it is organic to the story you are telling, great. But I am just going to make mention of it. Because these kind of character "hooks" have been done to death.

With the advent of the "Indy" film, the addiction or the dysfunction obstacle has taken center stage. If a character appears normal, he really isn't. He works at a gas station, but he is a Peeping Tom. If the character is a beautiful small town girl, she is probably a junkie. Or she carries a gun in her purse to rob convenience stores. The hook is she never remembers doing it. Actors love doing these roles because it allows them to play dangerous and chew up the scenery. But I think we have seen enough of this kind of obstacle, too.

Really good personal obstacles these days seem to fall into the questions of identity. Guy Pearce loses his short-term memory in *Memento*. He is trying to solve the murder of his wife. He is also trying to decipher the riddle of who he was. Emily Watson in *Breaking the Waves* is trying to comfort her newly-crippled husband. She is required to explore her sexuality to satisfy his voyeurism. But this was creating a mental split in Watson. She is also intensely religious and has regular conversations with God. She speaks God's lines for him. The movie is really playing with one of the classic dualism's, the flesh and the spirit. And as the movie progresses, Watson's mental state becomes increasingly confused. She is trying desperately to balance her relationship to God, her devoutness and her innocence, with the perverse needs of her husband. Watson is losing her grip on her own identity.

You see questions of identity raised as a result of computer mania. More and more movies are playing with a Hero's confusion over his real self and his virtual self. In *The Matrix,* Keanu Reeves is fighting his big battles in cyberspace. The problem is how to decipher which self was real . . . the guy kickboxing in cyberspace or the guy strapped to the chair.

What is my point? This is a new kind of character obstacle. Warring realities in the Hero's mind is a new and improved version of blindness or speech impediment or being fat . . . In another variation, a Hero's mind is invaded with visions, he sees himself in a time past or time future with a prophetic message crashing through, disturbing his present life . . . And, of course, schizophrenia is making a huge comeback.

So we are circling back to what I call inner conflict. You can give your Heroes any kind of ticks that you want. But the best characters are always struggling internally with a dualism, an old way of thinking and a new way of thinking. In other words, the best way to create a character is to do what Shakespeare did. Give the character a crisis. Give him something to do. And give your character a lot of inner conflict.

DETAILS

I have never articulated this until now. As we have discussed, a career in writing was an accident for me. I never studied writing, never took any writing classes. I had to learn as I stumbled through my own forest. I wrote and still write on instinct. So choosing a real acquaintance to model a character on was purely an act of desperation. Bottom line, I needed to give my character physical mannerisms, emotional needs, a way of talking, and a way of walking into a room. Details. I needed specific details. In today's Hollywood, details have become one of the working axioms that studio execs and producers love to point to. "God is in the details," they are fond of saying. It was simply easier for me to observe quirky, interesting details in my friends than to try and create them. And here is the real irony for me. Over the years, I began to realize that these seemingly quirky details work in a fantastic way. They serve as windows to the character's inner life, or as the poet said write, "they are windows to the soul."

ANOTHER TOOL FOR CHARACTERS . . . THINGS

This is an idea that has gradually taken root for me. It comes primarily from my experiences as an actor in the theatre. I started noticing that some of the world's greatest twentieth-century playwrights —Anton Chekhov, Harold Pinter, Tennessee Williams, David

Rabe— just to name a few utilized things, objects, (specifically) sensory objects as a means of negotiation between two people. I also noticed that these scenes contained some of their best writing, some of their funniest writing. As an actor, these are the scenes I love to play. In fact, one great scene like this in a play would motivate me to want to produce the play.

What do I mean by this? The thing is the centerpiece of the scene. It provides the motor for the scene. Our two characters will start talking about "olives" (Pinter), or "restaurants in Moscow" (Chekov), or the "Napoleonic code" or "faux furs" in Blanche's closet in *Streetcar Named Desire* (Williams). The characters are only partly talking about these things. They are really talking about much deeper conflicts, the rage and the pain. What they want to say to each other they are afraid to say. The thing becomes the argument. They argue over the thing. But eventually, what they really want to say comes out in a line or two. This is a great technique for you to use. And, listen, I am sure you have heard this advice. You don't want your characters to be constantly talking about the adventure. You know, "Alright, lets go over it again, J. D., show us the map" . . . Or, in a Hero and Enemy encounter, you don't want dead-on dialogue expressing their goals and emotions, "I will kill you" . . . . "No, I will kill you" . . . "You have five minutes or the girl dies." You get the drift? Boring . . .

So let's learn from the great playwrights. To me these guys are the true "Mozart's" of dramatic writing. I recommend that you begin writing your screenplay in three days. So I am not expecting you to go out and read their plays. I just want you to focus on this technique. You don't use it in every scene; you use it in maybe one or two big scenes. They are usually emotionally loaded scenes. You know you have these "scenes" in your own life. You are married. You are making pancakes. Your husband is an overly jealous type. He suspects you and your boss are having an affair, which, of course, is ridiculous. Meantime, you have become unhappy at his neglect for your artistic nature. He never wants to go to concerts, and he is constantly rude to your parents. Your marriage is in trouble. So he walks into the kitchen. How would a bad writer begin the scene? How about the classic, "We need to talk." Wrong. Boring.

Using the pancakes as the "thing," how about this kind of beginning?

HUSBAND
"You are burning the pancakes."

WIFE
"I am not burning the pancakes."

HUSBAND
"No, honey. I am not criticizing, I am just saying, I like just a little crust at the edge, you know, just a quarter inch."

WIFE
"Well, why don't you do it."

HUSBAND
"I am not saying that. I love the way you make pancakes. I love the way you look when you make

pancakes. It is just that you have started making them a little differently. You are letting them sit there longer. You are flipping them differently."

WIFE

"I am flipping them differently? Maybe I have had some influence in my pancake flipping technique?"

HUSBAND

"Yeah, maybe, I don't know. Have you been getting some pancake flipping instructions? Maybe with a new flipper?"

WIFE

"Maybe at the office? Is that what you are saying? Why don't we take a frying pan to the office and line up everyone who works there? See who makes pancakes this way?"

This is just an off the top of my head riff to demonstrate what we are talking about. But you get the point. You are probably thinking that you have seen scenes like this. And you have. Jack Nicholson's raging argument with a diner waitress over how to make his sandwich in *Five Easy Pieces* is considered a movie classic.

THE PLAY'S THE THING

One of my favorite American plays is David Rabe's *Hurly Burly*. I tried to get a production of it off the ground about twelve years ago in Los Angeles. But then David Rabe announced that he was going to direct

his own production at the Westwood Playhouse. That ended my dream.

The production starred Sean Penn as Eddie. Sean Penn later helped to bring the production to the big screen. In the movie version, Sean added terrific actors like Kevin Spacey, Meg Ryan, and Robin Wright. I saw the Westwood Playhouse production twice. I also saw the movie. I enjoyed both and I continue to enjoy the writing in the play. As a brief confessional, David Rabe, David Mamet, and Anton Chekhov serve as three of my major influences as a writer.

Read the play if you have time. There is a terrific scene in Act 3 between Eddie and his sometimes-girlfriend, Darlene. Their relationship is chaotic at best. There are many issues that pollute their attempts to get together including Darlene's affair with Mickey, Eddie's self destructiveness and drug addiction, and Darlene's natural state of ambivalence. In this scene, all of the various issues come together in an argument about where to go to eat. Eddie and Darlene negotiate their relationship by arguing over which restaurant to go to. Is it going to be a French restaurant, or a Chinese restaurant? There is a knock down, drag out fight; a long, hilarious, protracted scene. And the change of restaurants dominates the scene.

I also admire Sam Shepard as a playwright. I love his plays. In *True West,* one of Shepard's best, two brothers negotiate their differences by fighting over things throughout the play . . . toasters, screenwriting, the typewriter, the keys to the car.

MASKS . . . SHAPE SHIFTERS

The Ancient Greeks started this tradition. Actors were simply "empty vessels" to carry forth the message of the poet. So they would walk out on the stage wearing giant masks. If the poet wanted a character to become villainous, the actor would change masks.

As a young drama student at UCLA, I found the cumbersome masks tedious. As an aspiring actor, I wanted my emotional life to be the mask. This, of course, has become an epidemic with today's actors. It is not a story anymore, it is a Julia Roberts picture. Of course, the Kabuki theatre is also a tradition of masks.

Gradually over the years, I began to appreciate what these early poets were trying to do. At UCLA, my professors would drone on about the "unmasking." You, of course, understand what these academics were talking about. You have characters. They have a public persona. A public face. The drama drives the Hero to a collision point that results in a stripping away of his face or mask. Now we see the private face. The Hero is really a villain. The villain is really the victim. The girl next door is really a witch. The Wizard of Oz is just a little man behind a screen.

Of course we don't use masks anymore. After Joseph Campbell was truly discovered in Hollywood, especially after *A Writer's Journey*, Christopher Vogler's homage to Campbell, the term has evolved into "shape shifters." I cannot attend a story meeting in Hollywood without some young, attractive (usually *very* attractive) story analyst talking to me about the

95

need for a shape shifter in our story. Currently, this is one of the most popular devices that writers use to try to jazz up their characters. Create a "shape shifter" or two.

Certain genres employ this device more than others. Suspense thrillers use it. Fantasy, science fiction, and independently produced movies use it. But a word of caution here. You don't have to use this device to tell a good story. Movies like *Platoon, Three Kings,* and *Pulp Fiction* give us rich straight-on Heroes and villains. Half way through the movie, we don't see John Travolta turn on his buddy Samuel Jackson.

The Usual Suspects shook up the film community when it first appeared on the scene. It offered us a gallery of shadowy shape shifter characters. Suddenly a slew of movies, mostly bad attitude thrillers, started doing it. Writers began serving us surprise after surprise. It reached a point of absurdity in some movies. The Heroes, the Enemies, the good girls, the bad girls, all the characters were changing their shape so often that the stories were incomprehensible. More importantly, these movies were vacuous exercises in which there was no conceivable point. The only point seemed to be shock and surprise.

In *The Usual Suspects,* there was a driving motif: "Who is Keyser Soze?" The premise was great. The surprises, the twists, the ultimate shape shifting all worked. *The Usual Suspects* was art. But, most of the other films are not.

Where do you look for masks? Northern European fairy tales, Greek legends, the Tales of King Arthur all offer a splendorous gallery of shape shifters. A few years back, I became fascinated with Arthurian

96

legends. I found an English translation of the original *Questo del Saint Graal,* (*Quest of the Holy Grail*) written by French monks. It was translated by P. M. Matarasso. I devoured the book. Then I found a series of recent Arthurian novels written by Oxford scholar, Stephen R. Lawhead. I began to travel through these stories. The point is that King Arthur and his trusted mentor, Merlin, faced an overwhelming foe: Morgan, Queen of Air and Darkness. Morgan was the ultimate dark goddess, a witch. She could disguise herself as the most delicate, virginal damsel alone, in the woods. The lovely damsel attempted to lure Lancelot, Galahad, or one of the other Knights into sexual trysts. If a knight, especially Lancelot, yielded to this seduction, he would die to his conscious self. He would awaken in some hellish place. The lovely damsel would then drop her mask revealing herself as a hideous ugly witch.

These shape shifters are everywhere in our myths, fairy tales, and legends. At the stroke of midnight, the beautiful princess was now a cinder girl. The prince became a frog. The wolf was hiding in sheep's clothing. It is easy to see how you can play with these childhood metaphors and find contemporary characters that give us radical and shocking changes.

HOW DOES THIS TRANSLATE?

The examples in current movies should be obvious. Modern film noir depends on shape shifters. It is a predictable cliché. It is usually the female protagonist, the femme fatale. She appears to be a vulnerable goddess trapped in a painful relationship. She needs deliverance. Of course, at some point in the story, she strips off the mask. We see toughness, hardness, single-minded purpose. She has got killing on her mind. Our unsuspecting male is lured right into her crime. Sometimes the movie will take it one step further, or two steps, or three. The intended victim strips off his mask. He is actually working with the goddess. They are grifters. They have planned to use this love-struck male the whole time.

If you plan to use a shape shifter character, you should think about this. In recent movies, writers love to "reveal" their characters in very intense, surprising moments. There isn't usually a lot of dialogue in these scenes. We see it in a change of action. In *Memento*, Joe Pantoliano's character appears to be the Enemy, and a possible killer. It takes a shocking, violent scene at the end of the movie to show Pantoliano changing shape. It is the same with Carrie Ann Moss's character. She appears to be a nice waitress, a sympathetic ear for Guy Pearce. It takes another strange violent scene in Pearce's seedy hotel room. Now we see Moss changing shape.

A great moment of shape shifting occurs in the middle of *Being John Malkovich.* Cameron Diaz is the sweet neglected wife of John Cusack. She is bewildered by Cusack and Catherine Keener's obsession with invading John Malkovich's brain. Diaz decides to enter the crawl space. She is now seeing through John Malkovich's masculine eyes. Malkovich is having dinner with Catherine Keener. Suddenly Diaz is manipulating Malkovich's responses to Keener. She is feeling male feelings. She is attracted to Keener. Diaz becomes obsessed.

A GOOD SHAPE SHIFTER

The Devil's Advocate is directed by Taylor Hackford. It stars Al Pacino, Keanu Reeves, and Charlize Theron. It is a supernatural thriller. Like many thrillers in this genre, *The Devil's Advocate* makes extensive use of shape shifting. One excellent sequence illustrates the technique. Charlize Theron plays Keanu Reeves's sweet-natured wife. She is trying her best to adapt to the couples' move to New York City and Reeves's new job with Pacino's high-powered law firm. In this particular sequence, we find Theron shopping with two of the law partners' glamorous, bitchy wives. The two women parade around in their underwear in front of Theron in the store. One of the wives, in particular, insists on showing Theron her new, surgically enhanced breasts. This embarrasses Theron, but the woman is seductive and aggressive. She insists that Theron put her hands on the breasts and feel them. Suddenly, Theron watches in horror as this woman's face changes shape into a grotesque face of a demon. A pair of hands crawls up inside the woman's skin. This is shape shifting.

But this scene leads us immediately to a second scene. Reeves comes home to find Theron distraught. She tries to tell Reeves what she has just seen. But he begins to scold her about her emotional problems. He points out that Theron has chopped off all of her hair, which is the beginning of Theron's own shape shifting. But now Theron explodes into raging fury. We have not seen any of this kind of behavior from Theron before.

But the shape shifting doesn't stop there. Reeves begins to console his wife and agrees that they should pro-create. The two begin to kiss passionately and Reeves unbuttons Theron's blouse. Now the woman he is kissing is no longer his wife. She has transformed into Connie Nielson, the beautiful, charismatic seductress from Pacino's law firm. Reeves is horrified but he cannot stop himself. He begins to become ravenous in a way that terrifies his wife.

Everybody is dropping masks, or changing shapes in this movie as they all fall victim to the spell. Of course, Pacino is the ultimate shape shifter. He is the devil incarnate.

REVERSALS

Using big reversals within a scene is all the rage these days among young writers. I will mention it here again because I consider it to be another tool that you can use. What is a reversal? It is exactly what it sounds like. The scene begins in one direction; there is a surprise, an unexpected twist. The scene then travels in the opposite direction. To put it another way, your Hero comes into the scene with a goal. The Enemy surprises him or an event in the scene surprises him. Our Hero comes out of the scene with the opposite goal.

Television writing is really big with this device. Shows like *Ally McBeal* and *Sex and the City* constantly serve up comic reversals for the lead characters throughout the show. *Pulp Fiction* offers us a classic. John Travolta wants to taste the forbidden fruit. He takes out a mobster's wife, Uma Thurman. He is supposed to be protecting her. That is his assigned goal. Instead, he romances her. What happens? She overdoses. He is at the house of Eric Stoltz, his drug dealer. So the scene serves as a reversal to all the druggies who are there. They plan to party, but everybody ends up on the floor trying to revive her. This is the ultimate reversal for Travolta. Travolta's job is to protect Uma Thurman. Now she is about to die on him.

Finally, don't be concerned about creating a lot of reversals in your screenplay. Just tell your story. A lot of great movies don't use this device at all. Give your characters a purpose, some details, and something to do. Characters are primarily defined by what they do.

FRIENDS THAT RESONATE

Let me tell you my story. I experienced a fall. It was a few years ago. It began with a disappointing WGA arbitration. I lost credit on a movie, and the money I was counting on as a result. But it didn't stop there. Within a year, my father was diagnosed with terminal cancer. I was close to my father. Over the next five months, I watched my father die. Unbeknownst to me, my mother had signed over power of attorney to my brother during my father's illness. My brother immediately made several business moves that affected me financially. I went to my mother to plead my case. I discovered that my mother was not sympathetic. She had bonded with my brother over the years and was willing to give him total control.

What is the point of this little tale? I started pulling away from my old friends, my successful friends. I was suddenly experiencing total writer's block. It had never happened before. So I didn't know what to say to my successful friends. I knew that they couldn't relate. I began to make new friends who were also struggling with family issues and loss. I began to detach from my family.

This kind of thing happens all the time in life. People begin to develop friendships based on a shared opposition. In movies, you try to give them shared inner conflicts and old wounds as well. If you put three or four characters into your movie, each with a crisis, and each with the same or a similar Enemy, you have the basis for good friends. Each friend's adventure resonates into your main Hero's adventure.

What do I mean by this? You can cut to one of your friend's adventure for a couple of scenes. She (the Friend), for example, will go through her battle. Now you return to your main Hero. He is ready to face a similar battle. We as an audience will now experience with the Hero his battle, but it will be infused with a new intensity and deeper insight.

In *Boogie Nights*, there are multiple leads. Mark Wahlberg is the Hero, but he has many friends; Julianne Moore, John C. Reilly, Heather Graham, Don Cheadle, Burt Reynolds, to name a few. They all face a common foe - Family. They are estranged from their own personal family members. You can see it in the early scenes. Mark Wahlberg's mother is verbally abusive. She tells him that he will not amount to anything. Julianne Moore is crying. She is on the telephone begging for a chance to speak to her own son. William Macy comes home from work and finds his wife in bed with another man. John C. Reilly and Phillip Seymour Hoffman are so lost, they adopt Burt Reynolds as their father figure. Heather Graham never takes off her roller skates. She is dysfunctional in school. She hangs out with Papa Burt Reynolds, too. Don Cheadle is an African American so divorced from his roots, he listens to country music and wears country and Western clothes. All these Heroes share the same inner conflict. They are broken. They are lost and they cannot come terms with their loss of self. So, they embrace a similar absurd goal. They are trying to create a happy normal "Ozzie and Harriet" type family while making porn movies. The porn industry as "family love" is their new, shared Enemy. The obvious contradictions here are lost to them.

The point is the movie tracks through the different Hero's' adventures and setbacks. Julianne Moore receives a bitter ruling in court. She is deemed unfit to have custody of her son. This is a strong scene. It impacts and resonates into the next scene with the primary Hero, Mark Wahlberg. Wahlberg is desperately trying to forge out a singing career. The recording session is a disaster. He is treated with disrespect by the record company. He is basically thrown out of the recording studio. It is mysterious and wonderful how this works. A secondary Hero's setback resonates into the next Hero's setback. If we see a third Hero's dilemma, we are infusing it with the collective experiences of the other two. It has a cumulative effect.

In *The Sixth Sense,* Bruce Willis and Haley Joel Osment share a common Enemy, the Dead People.

But, their relationship broadens beyond therapist and client. They are becoming friends. Willis and Osment discover that they share a second opponent in common: abandonment. Willis watches his wife withdraw from him. She is beginning to see a young man at work. He shares with Osment his sadness and his sense of loss. Osment is ridiculed by his friends at school. Even his mother is losing patience with him. He feels abandoned. The movie tracks between scenes of Osment's alienation at school and Willis's loneliness at home. The scene of one Hero adds a richness and power to the other Hero's experience. This is a great way to develop and work with your characters. It doesn't require a lot of tricks or gimmicks. It is letting the truth build.

GOOD CHARACTER WORK . . . PUT EVERYBODY IN CRISIS

A lot of movies these days open with all the major characters in crisis. This is a powerful device. Do you want great characters? This, to me, is a great place to start. You begin your movie with each of your characters in the middle of a flood, in his own rowboat. Each character is facing a tough decision. Does he abandon the rickety boat, or does he try to keep paddling?

Look at *Traffic*. It has three main Heroes: Benicio Del Toro, Catherine Zeta-Jones and Michael Douglas. The movie opens with all three Heroes in crisis.

Benicio Del Toro is facing corruption within his own anti-drug police unit. He knows it exists within the FBI across the border. And he senses that his own partner is stepping over the line. He is facing an enormous decision. Who does he trust? Does he turn his partner in?

Michael Douglas is promoted to the position of America's chief drug enforcement official. But Douglas is also in crisis. His own daughter has a serious drug problem. So do her friends. You can already see a conflict, can't you? Does Douglas take the job, knowing his daughter is committing a crime? A former veteran also tells him that it is a pointless fight. On the larger front, how does he pursue his convictions in a pointless war with any degree of conviction?

Catherine Zeta-Jones sees her husband Steven Bauer arrested for trafficking. She is a complete innocent. This is her first big scene. Zeta-Jones is in crisis. What is the gut wrenching decision she faces? As a loyal wife, does Zeta-Jones back her husband? Does she take over his illegal empire and run it to help finance his defense case? This is a great situation. If she says no, she is abandoning her husband. If she says yes, she is committing a crime.

REFLECTIONS

Even in a simple movie, the Hero needs a friend who mirrors and reflects the Hero's adventure. In *The Man Who Cried,* Christina Ricci and Cate Blanchett share a common opponent. They are single women fighting for survival in a foreign city, Paris. The abstract Enemy is an alien culture. Ricci is a Jewish immigrant forced from her home in Russia as a child. Cate Blanchett has also migrated from Russia. To survive they take jobs as dancers. It is Paris in the late thirties, so a larger Enemy is also on the horizon, the German Army. Cate Blanchett meets narcissistic opera star, John Torturro. She latches onto him in desperation. Blanchett's attempt at romance with Torturro provides a strong contrast to Ricci's more innocent tentative love affair with Johnny Depp. And, of course, the two women later flee Paris together when the Germans arrive.

This is absolutely vital in all storytelling. You need the friend to have a reflective adventure that supports the Hero's main adventure. It just works in the movies. The Hero gains insight into his own struggle by observing the friend's struggle. And we as audience understand the Hero's conflict better, by also following the other friends' conflicts.

Look at the dinner party in *Notting Hill.* Hugh Grant's friends are simple Londoners like Grant. They work at straight jobs and try to amuse themselves with limited budgets. Grant brings Julia Roberts with him as a date. His friends act foolish, stumble over themselves, and are as intimidated by Roberts' celebrity status as Grant is.

Even Ben Stiller in *Meet the Parents* needs a friend. Robert DeNiro's son is sneaking back into his bedroom through the window when Stiller and he meet. The son has been on a secret drug run. The son finds the uncompromising DeNiro a difficult Enemy, too. I have mentioned that some writers allow their characters to share old wounds as well. What do Stiller and the son share? Sneakiness. And an appreciation of weed.

CHAPTER 10
THE PLOT LINE GRAPH

Here it is. I developed this for myself, and as a guide.

KEY HERO AND ENEMY ENCOUNTERS

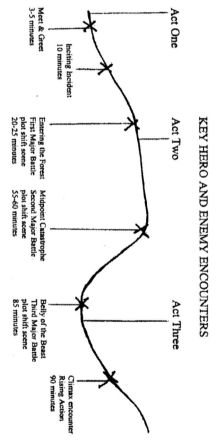

Don't let this restrict you. There are many roads to Rome. You can use the Argument, Counter Argument method. You can work from the Good News/Bad

News scheme. This is just one method. But it does seem to work with linear storytelling. Ignore it if you need to and let your own creative juices build your plot. That is always best. Think of it like a simple graph, the kind you had to study in high school. Or consider it a "stock market graph." Your story begins; your stock investment is doing well. It rises for a time, it starts to fall, then it crashes, it bottoms out, and then it rises again. Every story rises, falls, rises again. The magic "3."

Let me explain something, I developed this graph for myself ten years ago in complete frustration. In two consecutive, well-paying studio writing assignments, my plot line went haywire between pages sixty and eighty-five. I was lost. And I've got news for you - this is where a lot of writers get lost. So I needed to rethink my understanding of structure. I started watching every successful movie with a vengeance. Over and over, I kept seeing a similar pattern. It is a pattern of Hero and Enemy collisions. Some movies would have many collisions. Some movies would have less. But every movie would have three major collisions that would create shifts. In each of these scenes, there is a directional shift, a surprise twist, and an increase of jeopardy.

That was the pattern. It seemed to fit. Every movie was tracking this same path. I wrote the graph out on a piece of paper. This was going to be my map, my blueprint. I went back to my screenplays to rethink them.

I was teaching a screenwriting class in Hollywood at the time. I put the graph up on the blackboard and suddenly every student wanted a copy of it. I wasn't sure about it. But one enterprising student went home and did a very nice graphic reproduction on his computer. He gave out copies at the next class.

Hey, it's information. Technically it wasn't new, because this is what I was seeing on the screen. A quick thought. Obviously, some of these writers or moviemakers understand the pattern. Rent a video. Watch it closely. You will see this pattern in action. But nobody talks about it. Nobody explains it. Maybe nobody in Hollywood wants you to join the club . . .

Syd Field in his seminal *Screenplay* outlines a really basic version of the plot line. I was already a working screenwriter when I first picked up a copy. Alex Lasker and I were creating plot shift scenes in one of our first screenplays. But we didn't have a framework. We were working with some instincts about storytelling. We didn't have the terminology.

I was happy to discover Syd Field. He taught plot points and simple three-act structure to the world. He is must reading.

However, as I continued to write, I began to feel the need to find my own visual representation of a plot line. I needed it to curve. I needed it to curve several times. I needed to somehow visualize the rise and fall and rise again of the story. I also needed to build a shift into the middle. Why? Because I began to see that it is the elusive middle section of the story that sets up the Hero's eventual arc. It was only when I structured my own graph with the appearances of the Enemy that it started to work. And it does work.

Movies these days experiment with lots of devices in storytelling. Currently, ensemble driven, multiple plot line stories are big . . . *Boogie Nights, Go, Traffic* .

. . Some of these movies will tell three stories simultaneously with three protagonists. But watch them closely. If the story has three Heroes, each Hero will still have to have his own Enemy. And each Hero must collide with his Enemy in several plot-shifting situations before an intense, life twisting-collision of suffering and revelation. Then, each Hero must still have a final act. Every movie still needs structure. And simple storytelling needs one true Hero and one true Enemy. The Enemy must engage the Hero at a minimum number of points to drive the story. Notice I said minimum number. Your creativity can increase the number of engagements as much as you want.

Think of *Meet the Parents.* Who is the Enemy? Robert DeNiro, the unforgiving parent, of course. How many times did Ben Stiller engage him? In practically every scene in the movie. I have also begun to figure out that the more times the Hero faces the Enemy in a movie, generally . . . the more popular the movie is at the box office. *Meet the Parents* was a monster hit. Think of *Almost Famous,* where the young Hero, Patrick Fugit, is hanging with rock star Enemy, Billy Crudup, most of the movie.

Now, let us return to my graph. By watching movies, I have determined that engagement points occur generally at ten minutes . . . twenty-five minutes . . . sixty minutes . . . eighty-five minutes . . . and ninety-five minutes. This is the absolute bare minimum number of encounters you need with your Hero and Enemy to drive the movie.

Take a watch along with you to the next movie you see. I dare you. Time it. It never fails. I have been preaching this so long that scores of my former students tell me that they time the movie every time they go the theatre. There is a humorous moment I can share. Several years ago I was sitting in the National Theater in Westwood, California. At the sixty-minute mark, a big surprise confrontation scene took place in the film. Suddenly, in the darkened theatre, three flashlights popped on. These people were looking at their watches to time the event.

Think of your story as a boxing match. Each of the "Xs" on my graph are separate rounds. Round one is a "meet and greet" round. The Hero meets the Enemy. In *Meet the Parents,* Ben Stiller meets Robert DeNiro somewhere between six and ten minutes. Nobody wins this round . . . But in the next big round, at twenty-five minutes, the Enemy starts to gain advantage . . . Stiller discovers that his future parent is more than he bargained for. Stiller snoops inside DeNiro's private room. DeNiro hooks Stiller up to a lie detector machine. DeNiro wins the round . . . This is where the graph helps. You can create as many rounds between our main fighters as you want. But the key middle rounds . . . at twenty-five minutes . . . sixty minutes . . . and at eighty-five minutes . . . you need knock down drag out rounds . . . Each round should be more inventive, completely different, and bigger. Each round should also increase the odds against the Hero.

You can write your own story your own way, and go in many surprising directions. But when you sense your movie is slowing down, or lacking enough conflict, remember the graph and refer to it . . . Maybe your story is dragging in the middle. Maybe what you need is a scene of catastrophe. Maybe you need the

Hero's slide to take an abrupt drop. You need a scene that radically shifts the direction of your story.

PLOT SHIFTS

I mention this a number of times . . . Movies need a minimum of five major engagements with your Hero and his Enemy. Of course, the more often the Hero and Enemy engage, the more compelling the story. But in at least three of these engagements, you need a big plot shift. This is why I refer to these scenes as the three major battle scenes in the middle of your movie. The Enemy executes something in each scene that surprises the Hero, throws the Hero for a loop, forces the Hero to come up with a different game plan. In other words, it shifts the direction of the movie.

This is really vital, people. If you can figure out these three major shifts, you have gone a long way toward solving your movie.

A couple of quick examples . . . In *Cast Away,* Tom Hanks has several Enemies. Helen Hunt is one. The exploitative American media is another. But the biggest Enemies are Time and Fate. For a guy like Hanks, who is a big control freak, the Enemies of Time, the unknown of Tomorrow, and the fickleness of Fate, are big Enemies, aren't they? So what is our first big battle scene with Hanks and his Enemy? The FedEx plane crashes in the middle of the Pacific. This is unexpected, isn't it? Hanks did not see that one coming. It shifts the direction of the movie. It functions as the first big plot shift in the movie. It is the first major battle in the movie, even though the Enemy here is Nature. You should recognize something. The plot graph is strictly a tool to demonstrate the point where the majority of movies shift directions . . . twenty to twenty-five minutes . . . sixty minutes . . . eighty-five minutes. Some movies, especially these days, will use additional shifts. And, as in *Cast Away,* sometimes the shift will come from Nature, a death of a parent, or an accident. However, in my opinion, the best movie stories use the same major Enemy in all major battle scenes.

In *Notting Hill,* Julia Roberts is the Enemy. Hugh Grant is our normal working guy. Julia Roberts is a big American movie star. Hugh Grant meets Julia by spilling orange juice on her. A big exciting fantasy, but that is about it. But in the first big battle, Grant is invited to Julia's hotel. Grant goes to the glitzy hotel with flowers and big expectations. However, he is ushered into a suite filled with the press. Hugh Grant is treated as a journalist. He is allowed to see Julia for five minutes. The publicity man stays right there. Hugh Grant must pretend to do an interview. He is humiliated in the scene. As a capper, Julia tells him that their little kiss was a mistake. Julia the Enemy has stirred up the pot. She is royalty. Hugh is not. It shifts the direction. Hugh Grant's fantasy of a new relationship is seemingly busted.

Braveheart with Mel Gibson gives us a great opportunity to see clearly the battle scenes that shift direction. This is a war movie set in eleventh-century Scotland. In the very first scene, the British army is murdering the Scots. We see Mel Gibson as a young boy. He sees his neighbors hanging in a barn. Later, his father is brought home as a corpse. Mel Gibson grows into a vigorous young man. He has rejoined his

Scottish tribe. He witnesses an arrogant English commander demanding sex privileges with a beautiful young Scottish bride-to-be. In other words, every one of these scenes is a battle, but so far none of these scenes shift the direction of the movie. Mel Gibson's Hero (William Wallace) is a passive observer in these scenes.

It takes another appearance by the English soldiers before we see Mel Gibson begin to fight. Gibson is now wooing his bride, Catherine McCormack. They marry privately because her father doesn't approve. One of the English soldiers decides to rape McCormack. She and Gibson fight back. The English commander retaliates. He ties McCormack to a post and cuts her throat. This is what I refer to as one of your three major battle scenes. It forces Mel Gibson to engage. It forces him to give up pacifism. He rallies the villagers and they destroy the English soldiers. "Braveheart" is born here. This scene is the beginning of the revolution. This is a classic plot shift scene.

Again, this is a war movie. There are a succession of battles following this powerful scene. But the next major battle is not until the middle of the movie, the battle at Sterling. In this battle, Mel Gibson uses trickery to defeat a huge army equipped with cavalry troops. This is one of the few midpoint scenes where the Hero wins. It causes a shift in the direction for the Enemy, King Edward of Long Shanks. I will contend, however, that the true midpoint shift isn't until the next major battle. In this battle, Mel Gibson and his Scottish troops are defeated. They are betrayed by Robert Earl of Bruce and other Scottish nobles. These Scottish nobles turn their horses around and leave Gibson's troops to die. What is the point? If you choose to work with my graph, it is these plot shift scenes that you will chart.

A FINAL THOUGHT

Why do these five scenes need to be in your story, you are probably asking? Why do they need to appear at ten minutes . . . twenty-five minutes . . . sixty minutes . . . eighty-five minutes? The answer is, I don't know why. They just do! I understand them from writing action movies. What is most important is that these are the scenes that force your Hero to make choices. They force your Hero to make choices. The consequences are huge and they shift the story.

Start watching movies. Go to new movies when they come out. Rent videos and see them at home. Look for the major scenes and you will see them. You will start to anticipate them. You will know by checking your watch when one of these scenes is due. This surprise event will shift the story's direction in some radical way. And, that is the point! These scenes force your Hero to make new decisions. Yes, this is formula. Formula is generally the antithesis of creativity. But I look at it differently. Think of these scenes as your friends. In other words, you can have crazy pals in the movie, some crazy sidebar stories, pure funny outrageous scenes . . . but you as the writer can feel safe because you know that at twenty-five minutes you circle back and the Hero collides with his Enemy. Consider this formula. Gold. I see it in every movie.

Wendell Wellman

CHAPTER 11

THE THREE BATTLEFIELDS

These are the most important engagement scenes between Hero and Enemy. These are three scenes that you must create. These scenes create major shifts in the story. Each scene should inform the Hero more about his Enemy. And, ultimately, these shifts should drive your Hero and his Enemy to the third shift. This is a battle of pain and revelation . . . Think of these scenes as leading your Hero back home. What's home? It is a confrontation with the Enemy in which the Hero relives his wound. Going back to our graph, these major shift scenes occur at twenty-five minutes . . .sixty minutes . . .eighty-five minutes. In my opinion, these scenes demand your most creative plotting.

We can take a lesson from Jason and the Argonauts. We can think of the battles as tests, or trials. Sometimes using Greek myth as a metaphor in my head frees me. It reminds me that these big three battles are all different. They have different locations, different demands. They are tests. Another way we can think of the battles is in terms of music. It is a simple composition. You ask a question at the beginning of your story. This is your premise. This is your musical premise. Then, it is three variations on a theme. You want three variations . . . The German movie, *Run Lola Run,* did exactly that. It shows a young woman running through the streets of Berlin trying to bring money to her boyfriend. The movie is just a clever outrageous replaying of this same scene, three times. But, it has three variations.

Let me go back to a couple of simple movie examples. In *Meet the Parents,* of course practically every scene is a confrontation between Ben Stiller and Robert DeNiro. However, the three big scenes are:

1. DeNiro giving Stiller a lie detector test at the end of Act 1.

2. Stiller sneaking a cigarette on the roof, causing a fire and the destruction to DeNiro's outdoor wedding rehearsal.

3. Stiller returning a fake, imposter cat to DeNiro and his family.

As you can see, the three battles are three completely separate conflict situations. Each battle progresses in consequence and deepens Stiller's jeopardy.

In *Notting Hill,* the three battlefields are:

1. Hugh Grant going to Julia Roberts's hotel, and being treated like a member of the press.

2. Hugh Grant taking Julia Roberts home after a date, but boyfriend Alex Baldwin is waiting.

3. The media descending like a locust plague on High Grant's flat after Julia Roberts has spent the night with him.

How many times have you seen this scenario. Our Hero is a nice girl cop. She meets an Enemy. In the first big engagement scene (or battle), she fights with him in a traditional way. There is a shootout. The Enemy is too clever. He gets away.

Our lady cop knows something about her Enemy. He has a thing for beautiful women. Our Lady cop devises a new plan. She puts on a wig, pulls out a mini-dress and high heels. She is going to show up at his favorite bar. This is progression. This is what you are after, deeper and more personal engagements, from less personal to more personal.

I read an article in the *Los Angeles Times* by staff writer Tracy Wilson[2]. Basically it tells the story of Ron Bamieh, a young Ventura County Deputy District Attorney. Bamieh was obsessed with a nine-year-old unsolved murder. What was incredible to me, in reading this front-page story, was that I recognized the structure of a movie.

Follow the story with me. See if you agree that there is movie structure here. A beautiful young woman, Katrina Montgomery, disappeared after a party in Oxnard. The police found her bloodstained truck. They had suspects, some skinheads. But the police and the district attorney's office botched the case.

Five years later, Bamieh decided to reopen the investigation. It became his obsession. He recruited Mark Volper, a former sex-crime detective. They went to work. They toiled at night and on weekends since they had other jobs. It took four years. What is interesting for us is the number and variety of battles.

Bamieh started with Justin Merriman, the suspect. They isolated three suspects, Merriman and two other men. All three were skinheads. One of them was an ex-con who was willing to strike a deal. They literally walked him out of the prison under the prison authorities' noses. They wired him and put him in a car

---

[2] Los Angeles Times, April 20, 2001, pA1

with Merriman. Suddenly, Merriman got a call on his cell phone and he picked up their wire. He freaked. He realized his cell phone was being tapped. The con barely got out alive. Major Battle One.

Merriman later got arrested for assault. Bamieh and Volper wired his cell through a heating pipe. That didn't work either. Merriman spent five days in the slammer and didn't say anything. Bamieh brokered a deal with the second skinhead. The skinhead would get a manslaughter charge if he showed where the body was buried. He took police to the burial ground, but it was now a shopping center. No corpse. What a great battle scene! What a great twist and advantage to the Enemy. Major Battle Two.

Merriman was back in prison. Bamieh brought the skinhead inside. Bamieh arranged for two hot pants clad "ladies" to come into the prison for dates with the two men. He had the skinhead wired again. This still didn't work.

Eventually, Bamieh got his man. Merriman started to panic inside the prison and said things to another skinhead. Major Battle Three.

But look at the variety and progression of battles in this true story. It is as good as a movie. There is something else to see from this true story. Bamieh kept trying new ideas. He kept experiencing setbacks. The Enemy out-thought him. The parking lot out-thought him. This is one of the techniques of storytelling. The story needs a series of trials and setbacks; then the audience is instinctively ready for you to arc your character. If you don't set up enough trials and setbacks, the story doesn't arc. This is part of the magical mystery of storytelling.

I don't want to limit your thinking. Describing these scenes as engagements or battles is simplistic. Another way to think of it is as a lesson in polemics or the art of argument. Go back to the introductory speech class you took in high school or college. You developed a premise, and then you needed three ideas, exhibits, or points to support the premise. If your story is good, each of these major shift scenes will make a separate point. And the ideas will progress from the least important to the most important.

Christopher Nolan's *Memento* is a challenging movie. It rips apart linear narrative. It twists time and memory for its own purposes. Like *The Usual Suspects* before it, films like these are exploring the *"Roshomon"* school of storytelling. They are trying to solve a puzzle by coming back to the incident multiple times with new information.

Memento stars Guy Pearce and Carrie Ann Moss. It is especially fractuous. It is a movie whose vehicle is memory loss. You have to work hard to understand. Even in this movie, I spotted three big plot shift scenes. The premise of the movie is that Guy Pearce has lost his short-term memory in some horrible event. His wife was murdered in this incident. What happened there?

Again, I am providing you with a blueprint for three absolute minimum engagement scents with your Hero and his Enemy. Scenes that shift the direction of and progress the story. We will develop a separate chapter for each of these scenes. You need these scenes to build the structural spine for your plot.

So, let's return to *Memento.* Pearce identifies a piece of information at the end of Act 1. It is a tattoo on his chest. He discovers that someone has murdered his wife. He identifies Joe Pantoliano as his Enemy, but the movie shifts again in the middle. Carrie Ann Moss is a woman who is helping Pearce. A man attacks Pearce in his hotel room. The man is Moss's friend. Moss may be using Pearce as a foil in a drug deal. So now Moss could be the Enemy. This is the second big shift in the movie.

Later there is a third shift scene. Guy Pearce discovers that Joe Pantoliano is not a killer. He is actually a cop who is helping Pearce to exact revenge. Pearce discovers that he is using the identity, clothes, even the car of the man he has just murdered in this scene. This is a classic movie twist. It is the ultimate revelation. Pearce is looking at himself as the Enemy.

I think you can see that the simple, introductory speech class model applies well. In all examples, you have a premise. You then provide at least three different support exhibits. In *Memento,* the premise is who is the Enemy?

THE HERO WHO ATTACKS

There is an interesting point to make here. In a large portion of your stories, the Enemy brings the battles. He attacks. In certain kinds of stories, however, your Hero attacks. He brings the battles to an unsuspecting community, high school, factory, or whatever. And I am not just talking about "us against the system" crusader stories. Sometimes, the Hero functions almost as the Hero/Enemy. He appears destructive, violent, a bad seed, he flat out does bad things. Shakespeare's *Richard III* is one of the great examples of this in Western literature. He is the Hero/Villain. Richard is sociopathic, manipulative, reveling in evil; he is completely without guilt. But Richard is telling us his story. We are following him . . .

There are Enemies for this kind of Hero, of course. It is generally the community, the kingdom, in other words, everybody else.

So this is something you need to struggle with as you plan your story. Does the Hero bring the attacks to others? Or, is he or she the more traditional Hero?

Basically, we are talking about a Quixotic quest Hero, aren't we? The Hero appears to be the outlaw; he is being driven by some inner voice that is telling him that something is wrong in society, or his community. The Hero needs to take constructive/destructive measures against the norm. He needs to attack.

A case can be made for that in *Meet the Parents,* Ben Stiller is this kind of Hero. Isn't Robert DeNiro more reactive than anything else? As a matter of fact, Stiller can't seem to stop himself. That is the essence of the Quixotic Hero. He cannot stop himself. He is driven by some inner voice. He attacks everybody and everything. He attacks perceived ills. It is Mel Gibson as William Wallace in *Braveheart*. It is Meryl Streep taking on the corrupt nuclear facility in *Silkwood.* It is Ahab in Melville's *Moby Dick.* Ahab demonizes the whale. He leads his guilt-ridden crew to their deaths.

STAKES

I want to take one brief moment to mention something about "stakes." The engagements, the battles, have to progress the "stakes" between your Hero and Enemy. As a young action writer, I can understand this. In a thriller, a cop investigates a crime. There is a body pulled from the river. At the end of the first act, the cop is looking at another corpse in a city park. Only this time, there is a message scrawled on the ground. It is a personal message for the cop. You get the picture. How many times in these police procedural thrillers, do you see young action writers resorting to this device? The killer kidnaps the cop's girlfriend or daughter? It has become a cliché.

I will give you one more good movie example. Last year, I saw a film with Ralph Fiennes called *Sunshine.* It was a European art-house movie. Fiennes plays three generations of sons in a prominent European Jewish family. His father established the argument of the movie. He said, basically, "we are Jewish. By our definition, we cannot fit in. We are not like everybody else." The story was set at the time of European Nationalism. The Enemy was State Fascism, then World War II Fascism, and then later, Communism.

Fiennes' argument was the same in the roles of three generations of sons. He wanted to fit in. He wanted to hide his Jewish heritage.

Catch these progressions. In one engagement, he changes his family name to hide being Jewish. He is awarded a judgeship. Then he changes his religion. He converts to Catholicism so he can be a star on the national fencing team. Later he changes his politics and becomes a Communist interrogator in order to protect himself in the changing political order. He betrays his best friend. Three great and different ideas. Three major battles. Three major shifts in the movie.

Why am I bringing up an "art house" picture? Because I want to stress again that the terminology we use for these scenes is too limited. I am pushing to stretch our imagination. Let's think of these scenes as three different metaphors, not just battles or confrontations. We are back in our college speech class 101. We have a premise. We are now giving three support ideas or exhibits. In the case of *Sunshine,* the support ideas are family, religion, and politics. The writer builds three major set pieces, each one illustrating a separate exhibit or idea.

If we can start looking for the larger ideas to support our story, we will begin to look for our major scenes in a metaphoric way. It will free up our imagination. It will force us to progress the story, expand and travel into new and different territory. We will avoid movies that keep repeating themselves.

I loved Oliver Stone's *Platoon.* The greatest aspect of Oliver Stone's writing in this movie, in my opinion, was his creation of a "two headed" Enemy. Tom Berenger is the bad sergeant. Willem Dafoe is the good sergeant. They both function as structural Enemies for Charlie Sheen. This allows Stone to create wonderful scenes. Charlie Sheen is caught in the middle between two leaders. It is not just confrontation here. Sheen is caught between two sides of an Argument, two conflicting philosophies, of the Vietnam War. The scenes are set pieces of ideas. The movie is a metaphor. All of the major plot shift scenes grow out of the rivalry between Berenger and Dafoe.

HOW TO FIND YOUR SHIFT SCENES . . . THE GLACIER METAPHOR

To design these three major set pieces is a hugely difficult task. How do we go about looking for them? How do we ever truly understand them? I grapple with this puzzle constantly. I test myself daily. I think of a movie premise, or idea, in the mornings. I drive around in my car, go about my day, and try to see if I can visualize two or three major progressions. This much I know, the progressions must be brought about by the Enemy.

I would like to suggest that we use a metaphor. Think of a giant glacier of ice in the Arctic Circle. We are a small tribe that attempts to eke out an existence within a delicate ecosystem. The huge glacier sits fifty miles offshore, but it controls our lives. The glacier is the Enemy. And we know that there is a slow meltdown due to global warming. This concerns us and it affects little things from time to time. The yearly salmon run has not been as strong the last several years. But the warming is slow; we still spear plenty of salmon. Our lifestyle is pretty much the same as always. Then suddenly there is a low rumble that erupts into a horrifying roar. In a moment, in a twinkling of an eye, a huge section of the giant glacier

125

separates from the main body and sinks into the sea . . . Now our lives and our ecosystem are affected. Within a matter of months, we do notice the difference. The water is definitely a degree warmer. It is hotter for longer during the short summer. Because of this, the sea lion population is getting sick. Many of them are dying. We depend on our brother and sister seals.

A few years pass. Suddenly, there is another rumble, then a horrifying crash. This time a bigger section of the glacier snaps off from the main body. The impact of this split is like nuclear fission. Huge waves are rolling toward us and the water level is immediately rising. We don't need to talk. Everyone understands the message. We begin packing everything we can, dumping it onto dogsleds. One of our neighbors is lucky enough to have a truck. He will carry some things. We have to leave now. We have to find a new home. This gentle meadow on the water's edge will be gone within a matter of days. We must start over somewhere else. What will happen to us?

The giant glacier as a metaphor works for me. It reminds me that I need to define a very strong Enemy; an Enemy that is visual, powerful, and has a direct symbiotic relationship to my Hero. It is also a reminder that I can look to the passages of life as inspiration. A Young Man sets forth with a dream. He will be a great artist; he will create great works. But his Enemy is the greatest Enemy we all face: Time and Fate. He achieves some initial successes. He marries. He has two children. He learns the joy of sitting down with princes and kings. But, suddenly, one day, his son is involved in a terrible accident. He is paralyzed from the waist down. Our young artist loses years and money trying to find help for his son. This is the first huge breaking off of the glacier. Now the artist is forty, and he is struggling to revitalize a once great career. He suddenly conceives of a great innovative story. He writes it at night. During the day, he has taken over a job as a court clerk. His family has built up huge debts. He completes his story. He takes it to the studios. Unfortunately, a writing team had conceptualized the same essential story. Their story has already been purchased. Our artist Hero is just a little too late. This is the second splitting of the glacier. If you will think this way, you can begin to tackle these big major shift scenes.

THREE BIG SCENES . . . A FINAL REVIEW

We have spent a good portion of this book on three big battle scenes. People around Hollywood call them the plot point scenes. Some people, myself included, label them plot shift scenes. Each of the three scenes should offer a surprise, a new twist to the Enemy. They should force your Hero into new territory. They should be progressive confrontations.

In my opinion, you must define these scenes during your plotting. If you can nail these three scenes, the rest of your plotting is fun, easy. You are already winning. Now you can run up the score.

These plot shift scenes are not original. Syd Field in his seminal *Screenplay* first taught most of us that "plot point one" should occur at about twenty pages. "Plot point two" lands somewhere around eighty five pages in . . . but what Syd Field didn't do, what most writing books don't do, is to define the middle section.

127

What I have come to realize is that this is the key design problem you face. There is an old axiom that keeps coming up, "plot backwards." Plot from your climax back to your beginning. Well, I beg to differ. I say, "Plot from the middle. Design the middle first." You have to design this entire middle section during your initial step outline. The midpoint shifts the direction of the movie. There needs to be a huge surprise here, a huge dramatic shift in power. Now you as a writer have to shape the next twenty-five pages as the Hero's free fall. Sometimes it is the Hero and several Secondary Heroes' free fall. You as writer have to shape this section so that the progression of your story unavoidably leads your Hero to the supreme moment of suffering.

Why is this true? I don't know why. Maybe it is based on understanding the current film-going audience. How long can you hold them before you must deliver the knockout punch? Here is an important key for you to remember. This was another discovery for me. If your writing is good, the three battle scenes should be linked by an idea.

For a while now, all writers have understood that they need these big scenes. But in the last ten years, I have begun to recognize a new level of skill with writers. They are now finding a unique idea to link all three confrontations. I like to call this the controlling symbol. We will discuss this at length in the next chapter.

CHAPTER 12

THE CONTROLLING SYMBOL

There are three big battle scenes in the middle of your movie. They are all completely different. But there has to be a link. There should be one visual symbol, one image, a behavior, or an action that will link all three major scenes. You have to work to find it. This is the controlling symbol.

Obviously, the most elementary example of this is the "Macguffin". This is a term coined by director Alfred Hitchcock for the thing of a movie. In Hitchcock movies, for example, it can be the mistaken briefcase that Cary Grant picks up. It can be a suitcase of cash. The lost Ark of the Covenant. In J. R. R. Tolkien's *The Lord of the Rings,* it is the ring. Hitchcock's theory is that if you have a thing to fight over, it is easier to tell the story. But we are advancing as storytellers, and now we use a visual symbol as a grounding device. Sometimes it is a recurring action.

This is why I call it the controlling symbol. I have never seen any teacher discuss this. Maybe someone has but I have never seen it. The symbol, the idea, the piece of behavior becomes key for the ultimate revelations that come out in the big "cave" scene at eighty-five minutes. Sometimes it is the thing that eventually leads the Hero into the cave.

What I am really talking about is metaphor. How deep can you probe into you own psyche for a physical symbol? A photograph? A place? An event? A carnival that comes to town? A piece of property? A trauma?

An accident? What does it symbolize? Maybe you don't even understand all the conflux of feelings it brings up in you. Maybe you will have to think long and hard.

Maybe you will be surprised to discover that your father experienced it in one shape or form at thirty-two years of age. You first experienced it at ten years of age. Now, it is happening again. Whenever you revisit it, it is something that causes yearning, something that drives you, or reminds you that there is a mystery or puzzle in your life that you still need to solve.

Understand that if you find this powerful symbol in your own life, it still may not be enough. You may still need to express it as a larger, more exaggerated metaphor for your movie. The carnival that comes to town, a band of gypsies, a concentration camp, schizophrenia. Practically anything can work as a controlling symbol for your movie. Therefore, you can use this visual symbol to help shape your plot. What do I mean by that? It allows you to be more freewheeling in your storytelling, less linear. Whenever you return to this visual metaphor, it is a signal to your Hero and the audience that we are still moving towards a destiny. We still must solve this puzzle. The symbol recurs several times in your story. Each time it recurs, you need very little dialogue. The audience gets it. The Hero gets it. Yet, each time it recurs, the Hero is forced into deep conflict and thinking.

We discussed David O'Williams's *Three Kings,* a movie that I think is terrific. What is the missing link, the sustaining idea, the controlling symbol that appears in the big plot shift scenes? It is both an idea, and a piece of action. The Iraqi people are innocents. The sustaining visual action is that they are being tortured by the Republican Guard in each scene. The chief visual symbol is the innocent Iraqi girl. Clooney sees her in every scene. She works as a great metaphor for Clooney, Wahlberg, and the audience. It is a metaphor of America's Persian Gulf War effort. We do the bombing. We win the war. What about the victims of our military adventurism? What about the innocent Iraqi women and children?

VISUAL SYMBOLS

Some movies build their entire structure around a reoccurring visual symbol or action. *Memento* uses a good one. The movie opens with Guy Pearce preparing his body for another tattoo. He is also on the telephone attempting to make some sense of his crisis. This is fracturous storytelling with no sense of time or linear narrative. But the movie continually revisits Guy Pearce's tattoos. These tattoos are "reveals" that Pearce allows to be burned into his skin before his memory fails. Like a more traditional plot shift scene, the movie jump cuts back to Pearce staring at his body in the mirror. Suddenly, at the end of Act 1, a tattoo reveals itself. We as an audience have seen the inscription before but we haven't really "seen" it. It gives Pearce's Hero, and we as the audience, new clarity. Somebody raped and murdered Pearce's wife.

I don't want to suggest that one visual metaphor should always appear in every major conflict scene. To suggest that the controlling symbol is simply a clever bridging device is reducing its power. Sometimes it is a simple visual image. In *Braveheart,* a small Scottish girl gives a young boy a flower at his father's funeral. Mel Gibson, now a man, gives the grown-up Scottish lass, Catherine McCormack, the dried, crushed flower as a courting device. It is done with few words, yet it spans twenty years of their separation.

In the movie, *The Man Who Cried,* Christina Ricci is a Jewish refugee forced to abandon her Russian home as a child during World War I. She becomes a can-can dancer in Paris in the 1930s. A photograph of her father sits prominently in her room. The Germans invade Paris. She must leave again. She is now traveling on a ship to America. A German bomb hits the ship. Ricci is pulled from the water still clutching her photograph. At this moment I began to recognize the power of this metaphor in *The Man Who Cried.* The photograph isn't just a symbol of memory for Ricci, it is her drive in the movie. She tells Johnny Depp's gypsy character tearfully, "You are my only family." Ricci is looking for family the entire movie. She finds her father in the end.

Spike Jonze's *Being John Malkovich* gives us a great visual hook. It is the half-sized hallways, the lowered ceilings, and the long tunnel that leads to John Malkovich's brain. Not only is this movie one of the most innovative and absurdist efforts in the last couple of years, the sustaining symbols originate right out of our collective fairy tales. Alice tumbles down into Wonderland through the looking glass. The twisting tornado spirals Dorothy into Oz. *Being John Malkovich* plays with another metaphor, too. The puppet and the puppeteer. If someone or something (an idea, a philosophy, a cult) can invade the brain of a human, the someone or something becomes the custodian of his brain. He is the Puppeteer.

The poetry of film is especially freeing for someone like me. I got my start as a writer of action movies. Halfway through my career, I was struggling; I was having a horrible time letting go of the conditioning. Action writing is built on linear narrative. It is cause and effect writing. The villain strikes a blow. The Hero develops a counter plan and strikes back. More importantly, there is tremendous importance on scene-by-scene linkage and progressions. A clue here leads to the next scene there. You are always pushing the logic of plot at warp speed. I tried to branch out into playwriting and social comedies, but this linear thinking was not letting go.

This is why the use of a visual symbol is so liberating. Allow this wonderful metaphor to be a grounding device. Allow it to evolve your narrative and it will free your mind. Find the perfect visual metaphor for the story you are trying to tell. Then, let it work. Before you have written one scene idea on a note card, think this way, "Okay, here is my metaphor. How many different situations can I think of where it can play a central role?" I believe this strips away the conscious mind that screams out for moment-to-moment linkage. I believe that it starts to open the unconscious, which is fluid, illogical, beautiful, frightening, and dream-like.

How do you look for this metaphor? This another one of those techniques that you have to work at. Start looking at movies. See if you can recognize a recurring visual symbol. Start thinking about your own life. Is there an incident, an event that keeps coming back? Each time it comes back, are there different circumstances, so that the incident takes on different values?

MY STORY

I think of my grandfather's farm, a beautiful Norman Rockwell piece of real estate in Illinois. As little boys, my brother and I would go out to the farm with my grandfather. We would tease the cows. We would "moo" at them and then ran away when they looked at us . . . Twenty-five years later, I am an actor and screenwriter living in Santa Monica. My brother is a real estate broker here at the beach. My aunt lived on the farm, but she was crippled and dying. We flew back to see her in the middle of winter. I saw the land, but it was covered in snow; cold, lifeless, white. I sat with my aunt. She had been like a second mother to me. We didn't say much. She was lonely and sad . . .

My aunt passed away. She left her farm to my brother and I. At this point, the land still didn't make much of an impact on me. My concerns were with writing, the business of Hollywood. My brother and I both took out loans against the land. Then my father passed away. My brother decided that we were not going to sell any of the land because there were rumors of a new Chicago airport that was to be built. The land could eventually double in value. However, my parcel was under my title. My brother's parcel was under his title. I wanted to sell some of my parcel or at least develop it. I didn't have a thriving real estate practice like my brother did. I also wanted to get married.

To sell or not to sell created a huge philosophical rift between my brother and I. I made arrangements with a broker in Illinois to fly back. He picked me up at the airport. He set up a refinance deal for me. He wanted to put my land up for auction. I met with the finance people and the broker and I tentatively agreed to sell.

I sat in my hotel room later that day. I decided to drive out and look at the land. It was nearing sunset. Beautiful reds and golds painted the quiet land . . . The Victorian house on the hill was majestic. The farm had silos, cornfields, soybean fields. I got out of my rental car and walked along the road. A feeling of pride came over me. Suddenly, I was walking with my late grandfather and my blessed aunt. Their hopes, their dreams, I started feeling everything that they believed.

I called up my broker the next morning. I told him I couldn't do it. I drove the car back to O'Hare. I flew back to Los Angeles.

This is just a little anecdote from my life. But you can see that this piece of land, my grandfather's farm, could function as a controlling visual symbol for my story.

FORMULA

That being said, are there more formulaic examples of the use of the visual metaphor? Plenty. Even in a movie as quirky as *Nurse Betty* you can see it. Of course, Greg Kennear is the Enemy. His interactions with Renée Zellweger create the midpoint shift, and the low point of suffering for Zellweger. So in a sense, Greg Kennear is the controlling symbol. In other words, Greg Kennear appears in one way or another in the major plot shift scenes. But, what about the first big plot shift scene at the end of Act 1? Zellweger hides in terror in the bedroom as her low-life husband is brutally murdered. So where is the controlling symbol? The television is on. We see Greg Kennear playing his part on the soap opera.

Let's do a quick review of some of the movies we have discussed. *Meet the Parents* is a comedy. There is no visual poetry to speak of. But there is a sustaining action. Ben Stiller is being sneaky in all of the major battle or conflict scenes . . . We have already discussed that the victimization of Iraqi civilians is the dominant image for all the major scenes in *Three Kings* . . . Dead people have presence in all the major conflict scenes in *The Sixth Sense* . . . The behavior or actions that surround Julia Roberts's "celebrity" provide the basis of conflict in all major battles in *Notting Hill*.

In *Braveheart,* writer Randall Wallace is overworking the martyr or crucifixion metaphor several times in the movie. In the beginning, the Hero as a young boy looks at his father lying prostrate on a table. His father has been martyred for the cause. He is being prepared for burial. In the middle of the movie, Mel Gibson's warriors have experienced a bitter defeat on the fields of a battle. Mel Gibson is lying prostrate on the ground in the same physical position. He is broken. The Earl of Bruce has betrayed his army. At the end of the movie, Mel Gibson is in the same physical position again. Only this time, he is tied down. He is facing martyrdom. He will be publicly tortured and executed.

Why am I doing this sort of college paper analysis? Is it just to try to support my thesis in speech class?

No. It is to suggest that a lot of writers out there have figured out the power of a visual metaphor. Some of them do it poetically. Others do it poorly. The important point is that a strong and powerful central metaphor can be a tremendous help to you in structuring your plot.

SYMMETRY

One of the really cool effects of a controlling visual image is symmetry. Especially if your link idea is a piece of behavior or an action, you have a shot at some beautiful visual symmetry in an early battle and a late battle. This is why I chose to discuss the biblical story of Joseph. I love the classic symmetry of Joseph's imprisonment at the hands of his brothers. Late in the story, Joseph got to return the favor. He imprisoned his brothers as part of his plan. Audiences love this symmetry in story telling. It is the poetry of cinema. It works on non-verbal levels. You don't have to explain much. Audiences get it. The story is coming full circle.

The Thomas Crown Affair opens with an elaborate caper. Pierce Brosnan steals a painting from a museum. The movie closes with another elaborate caper. Pierce Brosnan returns the stolen painting to the same museum—this is symmetry.

CHAPTER 13

THE NORMAL WORLD

The Hero always starts in the normal world. This is his work-a-day world, his job, his life at home, his work pals, the bar that he hangs out in. A good book to read in your spare time is Christopher Vogler's *The Writer's Journey.* Vogler is really a Joseph Campbell popularizer. He gives us the fast food, McDonald's hamburger version of Joseph Campbell. Which is a good thing, because most of you have day jobs with little time to spare. But Chris Vogler isolates the various stages of the Hero's mythic journey, starting with the "normal world." It will give you some ideas. Again, read this book only in your spare time, because I want you to start writing NOW!!!

Let's take a quick look at the movie, *Notting Hill* with Julia Roberts and Hugh Grant. A great job is done with the normal world. Remember, movies are moving faster and faster. We have already discussed that a lot of movies these days begin with the Hero in crisis. *Notting Hill* does not. Even in a traditional narrative like *Notting Hill,* the normal world is accomplished quickly. It is the MTV influence, the channel surfing mentality of the Internet age. You have got only two or three minutes for your normal world: four to five scenes at best. So you want them to be up-tempo funny scenes peopled with crazy characters.

Hugh Grant introduces us to his neighborhood, an artsy, high-energy funky section of London. Outdoor food markets, funky hairstylists where people come out with hair "looking like cookie monsters." Grant has a roommate, a crazy Welshman who goes on dates wearing T-shirts that are blatantly offensive. Grant works at a travel bookstore in Notting Hill where he tells us "we don't sell many books." The bookstore becomes a visual metaphor for Hugh Grant's life. Grant is a low-key, average guy. This is also a running joke in the movie. The movie starts with this normal world. It takes three minutes, people . . . Then, in walks Julia Roberts, the American movie star, the Enemy. Two minutes later Grant runs into Roberts again. I timed it. He spills orange juice on her and invites her to his flat to help her clean up. He is nervous. He is excited. She surprises him with a "kiss goodbye." Grant is about to leave his normal world.

MEET AND GREET

Return for a moment to the plot graph. The "Meet and Greet" scene usually occurs somewhere between three to ten minutes. The Hero may or may not be in crisis. The Hero has already been offered his "adventure"; he is still debating whether to take the challenge. The Hero meets the Enemy. This is an important point. This is the only engagement scene that is not threatening. There is little or no jeopardy here. It is curiosity for your Hero at this point. That is why I like to call this scene "Meet and Greet."

In *Notting Hill,* we can see that the writers offer us two "Meet and Greet" scenes. The first is when Julia Roberts comes into Grant's travel bookstore. The second is when Grant bumps into her on the street. Hugh Grant meets his Enemy and enjoys it. There is no battle yet. It is mostly fantasy time for Grant. He is still living safely in his normal world. Be inventive and creative in your "Meet and Greet" scenes. You have only one rule to follow . . . the Hero and Enemy must meet up close and personal somewhere between three and ten minutes.

Look at *Meet the Parents.* What is the "Meet and Greet" scene? Ben Stiller and Teri Polo get out of his car in front of her parents' house. Blythe Danner and Robert DeNiro stand on the doorstep to meet them. DeNiro is already beginning his twenty questions. But it is still friendly, friendly. Ben Stiller doesn't know that DeNiro is the Enemy. Stiller is still safe in his normal world.

Important reminder: Push the envelope with the normal world. Give your Hero and his pals plenty of laughter and craziness and fun. Because the Enemy is going to take the Hero into exotic and life threatening places that aren't so much fun.

SET UP

The first ten pages or so of a screenplay is traditionally called the setup. You introduce your Hero, his job, his world, his marriage or his divorce. These days you also introduce your Hero in crisis. He has just lost his job. His wife just left him. He has just been diagnosed with terminal cancer. You also introduce the Enemy, as we have discussed. But, most important, you introduce the Hero's new goal, his task, his adventure. Sometimes I call it the problem of the movie. It sometimes appears as an accident. In Hollywood, we call it the inciting incident. But it is really a new idea. A new course of direction. Joseph Campbell calls it the Hero's adventure. It is the Hero's one chance to change.

In *Leaving Las Vegas*, Nick Cage is fired by his agent in the first scene. Then we see Nick Cage loading up on liquor bottles at the grocery mart. He is cleaning out his apartment at home. Cage has a new idea, a new direction, a goal. He is saying goodbye to his life as a wannabe. He is headed to Las Vegas for a final hurrah.

This is the most important demand in your setup. And it is part of your normal world. You must define the Hero's new challenge, his task, his adventure. You must define it for the Hero, and define it for us as an audience. These days it is done quickly and economically. It must prepare us for the ride.

In *Notting Hill*, when Hugh Grant takes Julia Roberts home to his apartment, sparks fly. Julia Roberts surprises him with a kiss. Hugh Grant has a new direction.

Like most people, I love J. R. R. Tolkien's *The Lord of the Rings* trilogy. I like to reread the books every several years or so because I keep finding new ideas that inform me. I was struck recently by the richness and power of the great council scene, "The Council of Elrond" from Book 1, *The Fellowship of the Ring*. Here Frodo and Bilbo listened as Elrond, the leader, and Gandalf, the sorcerer, and the other wise leaders of the elves, dwarves, hobbits, and mortal men spun the horrifying tales that surrounded the evil Sauron and the rings of power . . . Sauron knew that some hobbit had possession of the ring. War was mounting. The evil Gollum had escaped. This is the set up scene for the entire trilogy. Tolkien defines the goal - to destroy the ring. He defines the Enemy, Sauron, and his dark minions. The richness of Tolkien's details makes us ready for the adventure. Read it sometime. You'll see.

CHAPTER 14

THE FIRST BATTLE—ENTERING THE FOREST

The first big engagement is generally not a battle. It is more of a strange confrontation between the Hero and his Enemy. At the most, it is a brief "firefight." The Enemy offers up a surprise twist in this scene. Because of this twist, the movie shifts directions. The Hero has to rethink his approach to the Enemy. The Enemy is more complicated, and he is strange.

The Hero now knows that he is leaving the normal world, or his normal methodology. He is "Entering the Forest" in pursuit of his opponent. Going back to my graph, this is your first big battle scene at the end of Act 1. It takes place at around twenty-five minutes. This is a much-celebrated "scene" in Hollywood story circles. They call it the "plot point scene," or "plot shift scene". And, as we have discussed, there are at least three major plot shift scenes. In some films, there are more. This is just the first big shift.

What is important about this scene? It is a gateway scene. You all know these scenes. They come from fairy tales. Our Hero hesitates at the edge of the gloomy woods. Will he enter? Our Hero sees, for the first time, the exotic in the Enemy. He is surprised. He hesitates, but he chooses to pass through the gates.

Why do I suggest that it is a strange scene? It just seems to be the en vogue approach the last few years. The Hero has already decided to engage the Enemy coming into the scene. But this scene identifies the

143

Enemy with a trait, a clue, a piece of behavior that is unexpected and exotic. Remember that I have suggested that your entire movie should drive you towards the moment of suffering and secrets. Well, this scene is the first hint that there are secrets.

Let me give you an example of how the exotic of this scene works. Think of the countless "chick flicks" that you have seen, in which a beautiful Hero gets involved with an abusive man. He will play nice and court her in the first twenty minutes. What will happen in the first plot shift scene? He will start an explosive argument, hit one of her kids, or in some way show a mean streak.

THE FOREST

Why do I call it "Entering the Forest?" Because the Hollywood film-writing community is like a giant vacuum cleaner. George Lucas popularized Joseph Campbell's writings twenty years ago. Now everybody in Hollywood is influenced by Joseph Campbell's work. As Campbell points out in his writings, once the Hero chooses to pass through the gates, he invariably enters a dark, gloomy forest. Think of all the great Northern European fairy tales, or the legends of King Arthur. As soon as King Arthur and his knights elect to take on the Enemy, they ride out of the castle on horseback. They enter a thick, dark forest. Frodo, in *The Lord of the Rings,* goes on a great quest because of the ring. He gathers a couple of pals, they set out, and enter the dark woods. Entering the haunted or magic woods is part of Northern European storytelling tradition. Whoever our Hero is, he will usually encounter demonic spirits there. Ghosts, goblins, trolls, witches. In other words, the world of the strange.

The trick that all the pros use is to be very creative in this gateway confrontation. The scene should offer up the strange. It shifts the direction of our story. And the next few scenes they will write will be kind of like a forest. The Hero will encounter strange people doing strange things. Rent some videos, you will start to see this.

What is the forest? In *The Sixth Sense,* Bruce Willis is a psychiatrist, a man of science and reason. Haley Joel Osment is in a hospital. He asks Bruce Willis, "Do you want to know my secret now? . . . I see dead people." Willis is now entering a forest of the supernatural . . . What are the next couple of scenes? Haley is at home with mom, Toni Colette. She is asleep. The house suddenly grows dark, gloomy, cold. Dead people who are bloody and grotesque, start whipping through the rooms.

As an action writer, I think I have always understood this scene instinctively. When Alex Lasker and I attempted our first screenplay, we had no technique at all. We were writing a small thriller based on my college adventures. I pulled the screenplay off the shelf recently. I was surprised. We had pulled off a fairly successful first plot shift scene. It took place at twenty-nine pages. Not bad. We had never heard of plot point one or entering the forest. I think we just understood on some visceral level that our story needed some major torque. We were traveling in first gear; we needed to kick it into second.

If the movie is an action movie, or a big war picture, there is definitely a battle in this scene. But think of it as a brief firefight rather than a pitched battle. In *Platoon,* Charlie Sheen and his fellow "cherry" scout have fallen asleep. They never see the small band of Vietnamese "Charlies" creeping through the brush. There is a brief firefight. The Americans fend off the attack. Only one American soldier dies in the firefight. Unlike major battles later in the movie where both sides suffer unbelievable numbers of casualties. What is important for Hero Charlie Sheen is that he sees his Enemy defined. As a new recruit, he is introduced to bush fighting where attack is sudden and unseen. It can come at any moment. But more important he meets a new set of Enemies. Tom Berenger and Willem Dafoe clash over how to handle the incident. Berenger rages at Sheen and his fellow "cherry." They fell asleep while on watch. Dafoe rages at Berenger for leaving rookies on point. The movie becomes a power struggle between the "good father," Dafoe, and the "bad father," Berenger. Sheen is caught between the two men. So this scene is showing a larger Enemy, and is defining the Enemy for Sheen. He can't just be wary of minefields and "Charlie" in the bush. He must walk a tightrope between two soldiers in his own platoon. Of course, Sheen is already in the forest.

Ultimately, there are a few ideas that you can take with you into the scene. The scene should define the Enemy for the Hero in some new way. The Enemy is not standard issue at all. He offers an exotic and strange twist. He has powers that the Hero hadn't anticipated. He draws "first blood." The skirmish itself is a gateway scene. The firefight for Charlie Sheen is not just a baptism. It is a gateway into the thorny divisions of the platoon. Wow! By all reports, this was the most conflicted war America has ever fought. Platoons were divided by racial lines, drug users versus non-drug users, gung-ho warriors versus anti-war "freaks" and pacifists.

Finally, I have been talking a lot about inner conflict. The Hero forges a new Argument for himself in your movie, a goal. This drives him forward. The Hero is trying desperately to put away the old wound, the old tapes. But, as I suggested, this old way of thinking needs to resurface somewhere in your story. It needs to clash with your Hero's drive, his new way of thinking. Not all stories accomplish this in the first plot shift scene. But it is great if you can offer a hint of this inner conflict, too.

In *Three Kings,* Clooney and his pals find the gold. But they also see the Republican Guard torturing and killing innocent Iraqis. This begins a shift in direction. This hints at inner conflict within Clooney and pals. What is their moral responsibility in war? In *Braveheart,* Mel Gibson is trying to forge out a new peaceful farmer lifestyle. He has taken Catherine McCormack as his beautiful bride. He wants no part of the fighting. But in the first plot shift scene, the English attack his small village. They brutally murder Gibson's new bride in front of him. This is a powerful first battle scene. It shifts the direction of the movie. Mel Gibson will now have to take up the fight. But it also is a gateway scene. Gibson is entering a thorny forest. His Enemy is capable of committing atrocities on women and children. And it brings up an old wound. As a young child, Gibson watched the brutal killing of his own father by the English.

147

I mention *The Thomas Crown Affair* here not because I think it is a good movie. But I think the writers do a pretty good job with a couple of the major scenes. I like this first plot shift scene in particular. Rene Russo has already decided to take on Pierce Brosnan as an Enemy. She is determined to bring him down as an art thief. In this scene, Russo watches Brosnan deliberately sink his expensive fast moving sailboat. The boat "accident" jettisons Brosnan's crew into the water and knocks Brosnan from the highest perch. Russo is amazed. She is entering a forest of strange. Brosnan destroys a hundred thousand dollar boat for sport.

CHAPTER 15

THE MIDPOINT SHIFT

As an action writer, I used to believe this scene was a snap. I have heard some writing teachers refer to it as the "midpoint action." I've heard other teachers describe it as a "midpoint confrontation," which increases the jeopardy for the Hero.

But that was then. This is now. The new generation of artists are working metaphorically in this scene. The story is traveling in one direction. Suddenly, in one beautifully outrageous scene, the story shifts direction, reverses direction, it does a "one-eighty." The circumstances begin to implode on the Hero.

I took an interesting journey. I started to reread some of the great plays, from Shakespeare to Chekhov. It was exciting for me to discover a midpoint shift in these works.

In *Hamlet,* for example, it is the traveling players' show that functions as the midpoint scene. Claudius and Gertrude react with guilt and revulsion at the show. The scene identifies Claudius as a killer. The scene shifts the play. It creates a "one-eighty" shift in Hamlet's psyche. From a state of melancholy, an almost demented inertia . . . Hamlet experiences a surge of energy, a magical healing. Suddenly, he has clarity, a new-found masculine aggression, and purpose. The play itself switches focus from a mystery ghost story, to a revenge thriller.

This scene also implodes on Hamlet on another level. Queen Gertrude also demonstrates in her behavior a kind of implicit guilt. This is catastrophic for Hamlet. Going after Claudius is one thing. But what does Hamlet do about dear old mom?

Even in the subtle works of Anton Chekhov, I find the shift. Look at *Three Sisters.* The old way, the gentrified Russian aristocracy is collapsing under Marxist Revolution. But the sisters bravely hang on to their dreams. Polite dinners, the hope of Moscow, flirtations, and infidelities, the sisters will not look at the fires of revolt. The proletariat, the workers, the poor are the new elite class.

What is the midpoint scene? A fire! Suddenly, the country mansion is overrun with fire victims, the homeless, the poor. In other words, the sisters are besieged by their "Enemies." This is a catastrophic midpoint scene. I have been suggesting that most midpoint shifts in today's movies function as catastrophes for the Hero. As in *Hamlet,* the sisters experience a shift in their psyches as well. They must abandon their selfish pursuits and become caretakers.

MIDPOINT AND THE MOVIES

Let's look at the midpoint shift in some recent movies.

In *Nurse Betty,* Renée Zellweger's downtrodden Hero has an obvious inner conflict. She has slipped into a disassociative fantasy world of her favorite soap opera. She believes that Greg Kennear, the star of the show, is her real-life love relationship. After witnessing her husband's murder, Zellweger sets off to California to claim Kennear. This is her goal, or Argument.

When I read the reviews, I got excited. I asked myself, what will Neil LaBute and his fellow writers use as their midpoint shift? Because if the scene is good, it should play with Zellweger's inner conflict, fantasy as reality.

Sure enough, Zellweger finds Greg Kennear with his Hollywood producers at a Beverly Hills function. Zellweger begins talking to Kennear in a sincere, lovelorn fashion. The writing trick here is that Kennear thinks Zellweger is "playing" a part. She is quoting his lines from the show. Kennear loves it; he thinks Zellweger is a method actor, and that she is auditioning for the show.

This is a great creative midpoint scene. It shifts the direction of the movie, and serves as an opening up of Zellweger's inner conflict. It begins Zellweger's free fall. Greg Kennear is the Enemy. In every scene now, he is going to be attacking Zellweger's fantasy belief system. Kennear will give Zellweger a part on the show. Kennear absorbs Zellweger into his world. In a sense, Zellweger begins as the hunter. Now she is the hunted. Meanwhile, Zellweger is trying desperately to juggle reality with fantasy. It is pushing her toward a breakdown.

I was excited. It was a great midpoint shift, and it uses the metaphor completely.

MIDPOINT AS CATASTROPHE

I have already suggested this. I am suggesting it again, louder. In the last five years or so, writers have become very adept at this. The midpoint scene shifts the movie, the midpoint scene can do a "one-eighty" spin on the Hero . . . these days the midpoint scene is a catastrophe for the Hero. Is it always a fire? Of course not. But if it isn't a physical catastrophe, it is still a scene that devastates the Hero's goal, or Argument.

When the advance press began to build for the opening of *Pearl Harbor* in the spring of 2001, I got into a joking argument with a writer pal. He told me that he had heard rumors that the movie wasn't very good. He said, "The movie is too slow and the bombing sequence appears too early in the movie." I made a bet with him. I said, "How long is the movie, three hours? I guarantee you that the bombing sequence will appear at ninety minutes, at midpoint. If it appears at midpoint, they will do okay." Of course, the bombing of Pearl Harbor occurs at midpoint.

In *Titanic,* the ship hits the iceberg at midpoint. Catastrophe always hits at the half-way point in big disaster films.

THE SIXTH SENSE . . . ALMOST FAMOUS. . .
TWO GOOD EXAMPLES

In *The Sixth Sense,* where is the catastrophe scene? It is in the absolute middle of the movie. Bruce Willis is sitting in his basement office alone. He is listening to a tape recording of his therapy session with Haley Joel Osment. What does he hear? A dead man's voice is talking. For Bruce Willis, a psychiatrist, this evidence shatters his Argument, his belief system. It shifts the movie. Willis now must abandon his normal practice. He must work with dead people.

Cameron Crowe wrote a beautiful screenplay, *Almost Famous.* Let's look at Crowe's midpoint shift. An argument can be made that the midpoint shift begins with two scenes. In the first scene, Patrick Fugit is hanging with his rock star pal, Billy Crudup. Crudup gets high on drugs and swan dives off a house for the entertainment of a bunch of Topeka, Kansas kids. Crudup screams, "I am a Golden God". In the second scene, Kate Hudson directs her groupie girlfriends to de-flower Patrick Fugit in a hotel room. Patrick Fugit is hurt by this. He loves Kate Hudson. This scene is impersonal and sad.

Why do I suggest that it is two scenes? Because Patrick Fugit actually has two Enemies in this movie, Crudup and Kate Hudson. Both represent the rock 'n' roll lifestyle. Patrick Fugit's inner conflict is shown in several early scenes. His mother, Frances McDormand, warns him about these rock 'n' rollers. Philip Seymour Hoffman gives him a more direct piece of advice, "Don't make rock stars your friends. They are not your friends."

However, *Almost Famous* is a long movie. I am going to suggest that the real "shift" occurs in a later scene. Billy Crudup is in a poker game. He agrees to trade Kate Hudson and her girlfriends away for sex because he loses a bet. To this point, Patrick Fugit has hung onto the illusion that Billy Crudup and his band mates are his friends. But this scene devastates Fugit's belief system. This is what I mean when I suggest the scene is a catastrophe.

The true Enemy in the movie is not even Crudup or Hudson. It is the rock 'n' roll anything goes "lie." Fugit tries so desperately to believe the "lie," that he even accepts Kate Hudson's on-going affair with Crudup. He accepts it, even though he is in love with her. But in this moment, he realizes Crudup and Hudson are both victims, casualties of rock 'n' roll. They are not his friends.

The next twenty pages of writing are a horrifying stripping away of Fugit's infatuations with rock 'n' roll. Even Kate Hudson bottoms out on her friendship with him. "Why don't you get it?" he asks her. She doesn't get it. This is the heart and soul of this beautiful movie. It culminates with two harrowing scenes of suffering and shame. Kate Hudson on drugs in a hotel room, Crudup and Fugit in a plane "about to die."

DESTROY THE ARGUMENT . . . SET THE PATH

I've spent a lot of time discussing the middle of your screenplay. This scene is the crux of the problem. You need to think metaphorically in this scene. It is not enough for your Hero to experience a physical setback. You need to create an event, a confrontation or whatever, that works symbolically to defeat the Hero's argument, goal, his belief system.

I will always love the scene in *Braveheart* where Mel Gibson (as William Wallace) throws himself to the ground in agony. He is symbolically dying for his cause. The battlefield is littered with his fallen warriors. His ragtag army has lost a major battle. But the power of the scene comes from the visual action of betrayal. Gibson appealed to his Scottish noblemen to unite, to bring their troops. In the peak moment of battle, you see these noblemen and their troops elect to leave. Gibson and his rebel troops are left naked on one flank. Gibson is fighting for the cause of a free Scotland. These fellow Scots sneer at this cause. They betray him.

The midpoint should also create a directional signpost for the Hero. The path that he is following doesn't work. He begins a "fall." Inevitably, the Hero is on a new path. Whether he likes it or not, he knows that he is headed to the stronghold of the enemy. What is the signpost? The Hero is spiraling out of control, yet he is still moving in the new direction. What is his road map?

It can be a visual symbol that we see in the midpoint scene, and then it reoccurs in the enemy stronghold scene. It can be an idea, or clue. It can be an action that the enemy takes. For example, when cop writers have small imaginations, they rely on a kidnapping. We now know that the Hero must retrieve the kidnapped friend. In other words, the physical action of the kidnapping will payoff in a later scene. But don't limit your thinking to that cliché physical action. It can be any kind of unifying action by the enemy that you will later complete in the next confrontation. In *Braveheart,* we see Mel Gibson falling on the ground, symbolically dying for his cause. This action is repeated in the climax scene, where Gibson is tied down and tortured, literally dying for his cause. You are the artist. You can do anything.

SIMPLE MIDPOINTS

So as to not discourage you, I want to circle back to two of the simple videos that I recommend. *Meet the Parents* offers us an obvious midpoint shift. Ben Stiller sneaks a smoke, and starts a fire . . . In *Notting Hill,* Hugh Grant takes Julia Roberts back to her hotel. She invites him in, and boyfriend movie star Alec Baldwin is waiting. He treats Grant as the bus boy. This is simple enough, right? But in both of these movies, the Hero's argument or goal is under serious attack.

A FINAL THOUGHT

I have deliberately chosen a wide variety of movies in this book. I wanted you to see the infinite possibilities available to you. I wanted you to see how creative these filmmakers approach this section.

I recommend a simple exercise. Rent the videos of all the movies that we are discussing. Watch them only for the middle section. Note the midpoint shift. What is it? How does it shift the Hero's direction? How does it begin to expose the Hero to his inner conflict? Now watch the next three or four scenes. What happens in these scenes? Do they begin to point the Hero to his moment of suffering and revelation?

CHAPTER 16

THE NEXT TWENTY-FIVE PAGES . . .

FREE FALL . . . CHAOS

Anything goes here. I have studied this section. I have looked for trends, motifs, rules. Except for the sense that your Hero is floating through space, there are no rules. The Hero is falling. The curve of my graph takes an abrupt dive. Otherwise, there are no rules. You have twenty to twenty-five pages to play. Consider it your writer's "rule free zone." It is probably the most creative twenty-five pages that you will write. And you only really have to remember one thing. You must somehow shape your chaos so that your Hero and Enemy meet again at the bottom, in the Enemy's stronghold.

Listen, some movies really indulge the chaos. The Hero loses his job, his wife smashes the car, then she dumps him. The Hero has a friend. The friend is trying to help him find a loan shark. But she is also trying to save herself. She is trying to get her kids back. Unfortunately, just before the meeting with the loan shark, the friend is arrested for shoplifting at Von's. Our Hero bottoms out in a hotel room, drinking with a woman from across the hall. She steals his money, and his wallet. Well, you get the drift.

Some movies, like *The Sixth Sense,* indulge the chaos only slightly. Bruce Willis sees his wife kiss a fellow worker at her store. Willis tosses a rock through the window. But otherwise, Willis pushes forward with

Haley Joel Osment. He tracks Osment into a church, acknowledges that "dead people" are out there. Then we are on to the next scene, our two Heroes riding a city bus heading for the Enemy's stronghold.

You can do your section *The Sixth Sense* way, minimalist, or you can do it the big way. You are the artist. You control your chaos.

MULTIPLE LEADS

A lot of movies have multiple protagonists. One Hero begins his free fall, then all the Heroes begin to free-fall. The "trick" here is to somehow allow each Hero to share, in some broad way, the same inner conflict. What do I mean by this? Maybe each one is looking for family. This is the goal, or argument of each Hero. The inner conflict each Hero shares, for example, is family deprivation . . . bad family background, abusive parents, no love. During the free fall, everybody is experiencing the down curve. The stock market crash. The "trick" is to give each Hero his own unique and separate mishap. But symbolically, they are all sharing the same pain. Each Hero faces his own setback. The scenes land one after the other.

This is where you and your writing partner can be truly creative. Try to remember a down spiral. Choose a classic mishap that happened to you. Plug it into your Hero's scene . . . let your partner think of a classic mishap. The ruling idea is "family," let's say. Plug your partner's mishap into your second Hero's scene . . . come up with a third mishap . . . structure it so that one scene follows the next scene. The important task for you is to make sure that each Hero shares the same inner conflict. Each Hero should suffer similar results.

The discovery that I have made is that one Hero's "fall" resonates with another Hero's "fall." We as an audience infuse richness into our Hero's free fall by experiencing the other characters' sufferings. It accumulates in power. Creating at least one additional major character's free fall is one of the few "rules" that you should follow in this "rule free zone."

Even in a 'simple movie', like *The Thomas Crown Affair,* you can see it. Rene Russo is suffering late in the movie. She feels betrayed in love by Pierce Brosnan. She has seen photos of Brosnan with a beautiful young model. Her old way of thinking, her inner conflict, is coming back to haunt her. "She has problems keeping men." . . . Denis Leary, a by-the-book cop, finds Russo in a bar. He shares with Russo his experiences after his wife left him. He started drinking; he beat up a perpetrator. He got suspended from the force. He jumped in and out of one-night stands . . . So, here we have it. Russo is in free fall. In this case, Leary is in vicarious free fall.

Again, this is your writer's "rule free zone." You don't have to make it black. It can be quiet and elegant. In *Notting Hill,* Hugh Grant simply retreats back to his own simple London life after his midpoint. His free fall is quiet, albeit painful. The rejection by Julia Roberts and Alec Baldwin opens up Grant's inner conflict. Grant thinks he is totally ordinary, undeserving of anything special. The free fall is confirmation of his ordinariness. He is subjected to a series of blind-date dinner parties. He is not attracted to the women. He is lonely. He sleeps on his friend's couch. His Argument has been devastated by the midpoint scene. He no longer thinks that he can aspire to specialness. He no longer believes that it is possible for "a normal guy to date a movie queen."

MY STORY

I understand this section. I have experienced a couple of spiraling periods in my own life. Each time, an unexpected event triggered the free fall. One of these events was the death of my father. I had already immersed myself in the father wound literature. I had read Robert Bly's *Iron John.* I had read John Lee's *At My Father's Wedding.* I was reading Joseph Campbell's *The Power of Myth.* I thought, "Yeah, I understand the father wound. I get it." But I was totally unprepared for his death.

His death was one thing. The spiral that it began was profound. My brother and I stopped talking. My mother began suffering emotional problems. There were disputes within the family about how to handle the estate. My uncles and aunts quit calling. They regarded our family as a mess. I was affected economically. One family building put me on the brink of bankruptcy. Suddenly, in the middle of the screenplay I was working on at the time, I developed writer's block. It had never happened before. I just simply couldn't write another word. I lost all confidence in myself as an artist. I was chosen for a role in a low-budget film. I met the director. He wanted to put me on tape. I suddenly froze. This had also never happened before. I told him, "I don't want to do this. I don't want to act anymore." I walked out of the office. They all looked at me in shock. The woman I was dating lost patience. She asked for a commitment. I, of course, couldn't give it. She moved on.

For the next two years, I wandered around in a funk. I hit bottom in the free fall. I went from a working actor and a working writer . . . to a man trying to sell human growth hormone spray in multi-level. Well, you get the picture.

THE CLASSICS

Do you see free fall in classical literature? You bet you do. Think of King Lear, reduced to a lonely man with one aide. He was abandoned by his daughters. He gave away his kingdom and was rebuked for his generosity. He was wandering the cliffs in a storm, experiencing a form of insanity. He was no longer a king. He was a belittled, captive child, broken and lost.

How about Blanche DuBois in *Streetcar Named Desire*? Stanley stripped away Blanche's illusions, lies, and pretenses surrounding the family property. Blanche's psyche began to submit to fantasy. She threw herself desperately at Mitch. She fabricated the handsome, young man waiting for her in Louisiana. She depended on "the kindness of strangers."

THE CLUE

Younger writers are getting very skilled at this. They are using multiple Heroes, with multiple scenes of descent. These scenes can be wildly outrageous, sometimes profound. I am continually amazed at how they can navigate through the chaos and still have their main protagonist engage the enemy at eighty-five minutes.

When I look at any movie now, I look for the visual clue, the piece of business, the recurring symbol that we have discussed. Sometimes, this little road map is built into the midpoint shift. Sometimes, it appears in a scene after the shift. Sometimes the clue itself can be painfully simple.

I am going to give you an example of painfully simple. In *Meet the Parents,* the midpoint shift is the fire. The piece of business, the clue, the road map, appears in a following scene. DeNiro tells Ben Stiller to go find the cat. It is a command . . . Stiller doesn't realize that this action is his road map. Certainly, we as an audience aren't aware of it. But the cat caper is the final deceit for Stiller. Ultimately, DeNiro's request leads Stiller into his most painful engagement with DeNiro. In the enemy stronghold, at DeNiro's house, in front of the whole family.

In *The Sixth Sense,* Bruce Willis hears the "voice." This is the midpoint shift. He finds Osment inside a church. It is in this scene that we see the clue. They discuss what the "dead people" want. They conclude that "they want somebody to help them." They decide to help the "dead people." So, this becomes the clue, the direction that our Heroes follow. Next stop, the home of the murdered girl.

CHAPTER 17

DEATH AND SACRIFICE

Death is the single most profound event in life. I have always feared it. At times, I am terrorized by it. Every spring I experience moments of panic. "The cycle is beginning again," I always think. "I am still not married. I still don't have a child. I haven't done my world tour adventure. There is one year less in which to achieve my dreams. I have to push harder. I have to work faster. I have one year less to go. I am one year closer." Closer to what? Death.

I have a friend who is a close relative of one of our biggest male movie stars. She told me that "death has become his obsession." He buys great books on the subject. He seeks out some of the leading writers, theologians, and thinkers in the world for discussions. This movie star has since gotten married, started a family, and has evolved into the quintessential family man. I don't know if he goes to soccer practices, but he probably does. In the meantime, we don't know each other. I wish we did. Because privately, I have become one of his biggest fans. We share the same Enemy. We fear Death.

I began reading Joseph Campbell. I've read many of his works. He talks a lot about his own inner journey. How he began to study the great works of literature, religion, and myth. He makes the point that recurring themes and stories appear in every culture. The Great Flood (the story of Noah and the Ark), for example, isn't just a Judeo-Christian tale. This story of

163

world catastrophe appears in the mythology of every culture. What is this story of the Flood? It is the story of a lot of people dying.

Death is the ultimate passage for every Hero. In the Bible, there is a recurring metaphor: "seed time and harvest." A seed is planted in the ground, it dies. The seed's "death" in the ground brings forth new life, a living plant. What is the point of this metaphor for us as writers? Transformation comes from the act of death.

In his book, *The Power of Myth,* Joseph Campbell is fascinated by ancient tribal initiation rites. The young men of the tribe are uprooted, thrown into the forest for a brutal hell week. Their front teeth are knocked out. They are initiated through pain and suffering. Their childhood dies in the forest. The shattered teeth sink into the ground along with their innocence. Death brings forth new life. The child becomes a man. A warrior. A member of the tribe.

What is the point of this discussion? Death is your most important tool in writing. Ultimately your Hero must come face to face with death. Violence and death drives audiences to line up for Morgan Freeman suspense thrillers, or *Saving Private Ryan.* Death is the centerpiece of blockbusters like *Titanic, Gladiator,* and *Pearl Harbor*. It is the ticking time bomb that allows audience to laugh at all of the "badda bing!" shenanigans of *The Sopranos.* Death is the ultimate writers' weapon in every story. Death is in comedies. Death drives "chick flicks." Maybe it isn't a physical death. But somewhere in the middle of the movie, a romance disintegrates. Maybe later in the movie, a parent passes away.

I had a discussion with a writing pal recently. I said, "I love World War II movies. I am glad we are having another run of them because the Nazis were the most horrific Enemy mankind has ever faced.

What is the Argument that drives these stories? Freedom and hope. You don't have to see the violence. The threat of it frames every moment of the story and gives these stories their power. These Heroes elicit our compassion. These Heroes have a dimension and richness that Heroes in many other stories do not. The Enemy, Death, is hovering over them like a cloud every minute.

Again, what is the point of this discussion? The third battle scene in your story, which follows the Hero's free fall. is a scene where your Hero faces death. It is a death scene. You probably already know this. Almost everybody does. We learn to expect it. My writing partner, Alex Lasker and I knew this. At least, we knew it instinctively. We were young writers so sometimes we resorted to cliché, grotesque violence. However, in the movie *Firefox,* we got it right. The scene is set in the hangar that houses the Russian spy plane. Clint Eastwood is upstairs in his Russian flight uniform. He knows that the mechanics in the hangar below are going to die for the cause. The delayed stress overwhelms him. He has an flashback. All of his horrible war memories come flooding back. The flight mechanics downstairs are going to sacrifice themselves for Eastwood's Hero.

Over the years I have grappled with this scene. I have studied it. I have tried to make it my key scene in my screenplays. I teach it in writing classes. I sometimes call it the "cave" scene. This label comes from Joseph Campbell. I also call it the "belly of the beast."

BELLY OF THE BEAST

Everybody knows the genesis of this metaphor. It is another Old Testament story. Jonah was a man of God. But he was rebelling against God's call. God wanted Jonah to go to Ninevah and preach to the people there. Jonah didn't want to go to Ninevah. He thought the city was too wicked and should burn. So Jonah went to sea. Using our writer's terminology, this was Jonah's argument. He could still be a man of God, but he could exercise free will. Well, a storm kicked up at sea. The sailors were about to die. Jonah confessed that he rebelled against God. The sailors appreciated his honesty and threw him overboard. Jonah was swallowed by a whale. He survived in this womb-like nightmare for three days. In a sense, he was in a death state for three days. Interestingly enough, Christ was in the tomb—a death state—for three days. Then the whale coughed Jonah up. Jonah was in a state of rebellion when he was swallowed by the whale. The whale now spat out a man transformed. The whale spat out a prophet.

If you look at this metaphor, you should begin to understand what we are trying to accomplish with this scene. It a death scene in metaphoric terms.

Over the years, I have always understood this scene on some level. But it is a mystery scene. In some movies, we don't understand why a parent dying at the end of Act 2 creates such a cathartic effect in the audience. But it does. We can see it in the theatre. You

166

know what I am talking about. Suddenly, the audience grows very quiet. The next few scenes begin to affect them. The Hero begins a transformation. The death scene arcs the character. . .the death scene arcs the story. It is the basis of all dramatic writing. It is the centerpiece of theology. It is the basis of all storytelling. Through death, we find new life.

Thank you for indulging my grad school meditation. I just wanted you to think metaphorically as we approach the scene. Your scene does not have to be that heavy. If you are writing a romantic comedy, obviously you are not going to have someone dying in the "belly of the beast." In *Meet the Parents,* this scene is a confrontation scene between Stiller and DeNiro. Stiller has painted the cat's tail. DeNiro exposes Stiller's lie. The whole family looks on. It is humiliating. It is funny. Stiller is sneaky. DeNiro is sneaky. That's it. The scene is just dialogue. Nothing more. Nothing less.

So you are probably thinking, how is this a cave scene? It takes place in DeNiro's house. DeNiro is the Enemy. Stiller sees a powerful revelation about his Enemy. DeNiro is sneaky, too. You are thinking, where is the death? What is dying in the scene is Stiller's self deception. His Argument is dying. "I can be a sneaky geeky guy and not adapt to a family's ways and still take home the princess." His inner conflict, his old way of thinking that he doesn't feel worthy, comes flashing back. Stiller sees it and, what's worse, everybody else sees it. Stiller is publicly humiliated. A public humiliation is a form of dying, isn't it? And, of course, Stiller looks at Teri Polo. She is viewing him with sadness. Their romance is falling apart, too.

A lot of movies these days do nothing more than this. They offer you a big confrontation scene between the Hero and his or her Opponent. It could be the lover in a romantic comedy. It could be the mother in a family film.

In the movie, *Pay It Forward*, it is a simple scene between Kevin Spacey and Helen Hunt in a supermarket parking lot. Spacey is backed into a corner here. Hunt is forcing Spacey to confront why he has run from the relationship. Spacey destroys Hunt's illusions right here. He begins telling Hunt of the secret behind his scars. His father deliberately threw gasoline on Spacey as a boy. The father lit a match. Kevin Spacey may be too emotionally scarred to receive love.

Understand, you are again free to create whatever kind of scene you choose. What is important for you to remember is that the truth comes out in this scene. Secrets come to light here. Your entire movie has been moving your Hero to this moment. We will learn the truth about his Enemy. And the Hero begins to see the truth about himself, and his illusions. I suggested that this is the most important scene in your movie; it arcs your Hero's character. I want to qualify this statement. It begins the arc. The Hero has a few more events to go through before he changes. But the change begins here. This is the catalyst. The truth comes out here. It devastates him. He suffers in this scene.

I want to pause for a moment. Let's do a quick review of one of your key elements. The scene generally takes place in the Enemy's world. It doesn't have to be his house. It could be anywhere, but it brings to light who the Enemy is. In any movie, romantic comedy, a caper film, an "Academy Award" type film - the Hero is still trying to solve a puzzle about his or her Enemy. Truth is brought to light here. Secrets are revealed. It is easy to get to that "truth" if you see the enemy in his environment, doing what he does. In *Notting Hill,* the scene takes place in Hugh Grant's flat. But hoards of the press are just outside the door. The movie industry paparazzi are like slimy monsters crawling against the door. So, it is really the Enemy's turf. Julia Roberts is angry, but she really revels in it. She needs the press. The press needs her. Hugh Grant sees the truth of Julia Roberts for the first time. The second important element we have already touched on. In this same event, something in the Hero "dies." His Argument and way of thinking dies here. Whatever the Hero is hoping for, whatever the Hero wants to believe is shattered. The Hero suffers, he hurts, he is broken.

Let us take a look at action movies and thrillers for a moment. Many times, these movies resort to clichés. They have a gruesome body they dig up. Or, the Hero is tortured, and beaten in the scene. In *Lethal Weapon,* Mel Gibson is hanging from the ceiling. He is suffering a severe beating in the scene. Some of these movies also resort to the overt clichés of the cave concept. In serial killer police thrillers, how many times have you seen our cop Heroes wandering through dark, smelly basements with flashlights? They are in the cave of the psycho killer. They find some gruesome pictures and body parts. In *Double Jeopardy,* I had to laugh. The writers are so obsessed with creating "Cave imagery" that they put Ashley Judd in a dark, smelly casket with a rotting corpse. The scene works on a physical level, but it doesn't work on an idea level. There is no meaningful dialogue. There is suffering, but no true confrontation. Truths are not coming out.

Contrast these examples with a truly intelligent action adventure like *Three Kings.* Mark Wahlberg is bound and being tortured by the Republican Guards. We are in a smelly, dusty Enemy bunker. Okay, this is the cliché cave and our Hero is suffering. But take a look at what is really going on here. It is a confrontation scene. Wahlberg's interrogator is a nice looking Iraqi soldier. He tells Wahlberg that American bombs murdered his wife and child. He asks Wahlberg if he has a wife and child. Suddenly, Wahlberg visualizes his own wife and child being murdered by bombs. Wahlberg is devastated. He sees the truth of war. There are victims on both sides. Wahlberg sees the truth of his Enemy. They are the same. Wahlberg's way of thinking begins to crumble. "Americans are always right in war. We don't have to worry about the collateral damage from our smart bombs. We can also steal a little gold while we are at it, too." This is a great scene. This is an example of death and sacrifice. The wives and children are the sacrificial lambs of war.

Let's take a look at this scene in two more movies. In *The Sixth Sense,* Bruce Willis and Haley Joel Osment go to the house of the Enemy. A wake is in progress for the dead girl who is crying out for help. Osment finds the dead girl under her bed. She gives him a video. Willis and Osment watch as the father plays the video . . . The truth comes out. In public with everyone watching, the stepmother is exposed. She was giving the little girl medicine to keep her sick. Death is present in this scene on many levels. For the father, it is the death of his daughter and the truth about his marriage. For Haley Joel Osment, it is really a scene of freedom. Finally, the dead people who have tortured him will let him go. For Bruce Willis, it is the final death of his career as a psychiatrist.

In the very next scene, Haley Joel Osment performs in a play. Osment is okay, now. Willis tells him, "We won't be meeting anymore." There is more than a little sadness here, for both our Heroes. Of course, both of our Heroes have one more scene of truth and revelation yet to go. With Haley, it is a scene with his mother. For Willis, it is a scene with his wife.

One final thought, I mentioned the concept of sacrifice. Is it present in every movie? No. I can't really think of a sacrifice in *Notting Hill* or *Meet the Parents*. But it is present in *The Sixth Sense* in this scene. The truth comes to light. The little girl is murdered. She wants her story told. By experiencing vicariously the little girl's death and suffering, Haley Joel Osment and Bruce Willis can be healed. The little girl's death functions as the sacrifice. Returning to my "Grad Student" meditation, her death brings life to Osment and Willis.

Is the concept of sacrifice important? The sacrament of the Last Supper, which is symbolic of Christ's death, is one of the central and dominant motifs of much of Western art. As we have discussed, even non-Christian art relies on sacrificial symbols, seed time and harvest, killing a beast for food, etc. The point I am making here is that you do not always need a physical death scene at the end of Act 2 in order to convey sacrifice and growth.

SCENE OF SACRIFICE . . .
DOES IT ALWAYS WORK? DO YOU NEED IT?

Campbell did a series of PBS interviews fourteen years ago, and George Lucas made him the Patron Saint of the *Star Wars* trilogy. Hollywood really jumped on the bandwagon. Practically every writer in town was grabbing acts of sacrifice and jamming them into their plot line. As we would approach the eighty-five minute mark of a film, I would check my watch. I would know that either preceding or following the cave scene, a good person, a friend of the Hero, would die. It became another cliché. It became gratuitous.

Do you need this scene? Only if your story needs this scene. Don't do it just to get a rise out of the audience. As I pointed out, *Meet the Parents* doesn't really offer us an act of sacrifice, unless you count the cat who disappeared. It is not a great movie. But it is a hit. Audiences like it. Audiences didn't like it in *Pay It Forward,* for example. This movie offers a big martyr's death for Haley Joel Osment.

When I was lecturing at Storyboard, one particular evening, we were analyzing the screenplay of *Pay It Forward.* There were probably thirty-five people in attendance. I would say that eighty percent of the participants hated seeing Haley Joel Osment die. They felt it was contrived. They felt manipulated. The movie, of course, did a big zero at the box office. Again, your job is to decide whether the truth of your story dictates a car accident for Grandma.

EFFECTIVE USE OF SACRIFICE

There is an argument that a scene of sacrifice is still essential. If you are in a particular kind of bondage in your life, sometimes it takes something powerful to release you. A death of someone, especially if their death comes from the blindness or the folly of your kind of thinking, will sometimes free your eyes from their scales.

The important point here is that if you are going to use a scapegoat character in your story, you need to set him up clearly in your story outline. You need to determine his relationship to the Hero. We need to see it early on. You need to decide how this character's death reflects the folly of your Hero's argument. In some stories, the sidebar character embraces the same faulty thinking. In other stories, he is purely an accidental victim of the Hero's goals and thinking. In either case, the Hero will see a mirror reflection of himself in the character's sacrificial death.

One point you should keep in mind. If you are going to use a scene of "sacrifice," it is generally a separate small scene, proceeding or immediately following the "cave" sequence. And the two scenes work together to help create your Hero's "moment" of change.

I recognized this pattern at work beautifully in Neil Slaven's *Focus,* starring William Macy, Laura Dern, and David Paymer. As a quick review, William Macy and Laura Dern are trying desperately to deny their Jewish heritage or appearance.

William Macy is brought "low" in the beating scene. His attempts at assimilation with the thugs of his neighborhood bring him to this moment of pain and humiliation. He suffers a severe beating at the hands of the very people he is trying to embrace. This is a very powerful technique. So I will put it another way. Using our terminology of a Hero's argument, Macy is defeated by what he tries to embrace.

As a further humiliation, David Paymer becomes the only man to defend Macy. Paymer is a fellow victim.

Here is the key point. The transformation doesn't occur in the scene itself. As we have discussed, it sometimes requires several scenes in succession. The very next scene takes place in Paymer's store. Macy is still clinging to his initial argument. Macy implores Paymer to move out of the neighborhood for his own protection. But Paymer refuses. Paymer will not be intimidated.

In the very first scene in the movie, we see Macy watching a woman being raped and brutalized outside his window. Macy chooses not to get involved, nor to report it to the police. This is a metaphor for Macy's inner conflict. He is a mother-dominated passive male who can't or won't stand up in life. Paymer now gives Macy the "news." Paymer has been visiting the woman in the hospital. The woman has just died as a result of her injuries.

Macy reacts to the news with shame and recognition. The woman's death functions as the sacrificial act. But something else is happening here. The reality of the woman's death results in a duplication of Macy's cowardly behavior that we see in the beginning. Remember that we are hoping to bring a clash of the Hero's argument and his inner conflict into one major battle scene. The news of the woman's death creates the "moment" of change for Macy.

Notice that it is two scenes working together. The beating and the news of the woman's death are both necessary. The act of sacrifice is not manipulative. The woman's tragedy begins the movie. And the progression of her tragedy here provides a powerful revelation.

CHAPTER 18

REUNION, THE WEDDING, FLIGHT . . . YOUR CLIMAX

The climax in movies is really undergoing change. Traditionally, you expect a *Rocky* type ending. A big grand finale in the ring. A series of car crashes, horrific explosions, Gary Busey and Mel Gibson beating each other's face in as in *Lethal Weapon.* Thankfully, this era is at an end. If the eighties and early nineties was into the "big bang," the new millennium offers us the quiet ripple.

What has changed? First, the younger generation of writers really arc their Hero's journey and all other characters' journeys in brilliantly conceived scenes, virtuoso scenes between the midpoint shift and the end of Act 2. We have already discussed this. The audience has already experienced great suffering and great catharsis and insight with their Heroes. They don't need to be pummeled again. Secondly, the Hero's old way of thinking has been wiped out. He sees his inner conflict now. He is "getting it." And, if the Hero's own "epiphany" isn't quite enough, a secondary Hero's mirror "epiphany" completes the lesson. As a consequence, third acts in today's films play relatively short.

This is not meant to confuse you. The Heroes still must face the Enemy in a final battle. But in most movies these days, it is a quieter battle. It is more about letting go. Freedom. What do I mean by that? It is a final test for the Hero. It is an opportunity for him to make a new decision, not cluttered by his inner conflict.

So what do you look for in building your climax? Again, I made this discovery by watching movies, and rethinking classic mythic structure. Eventually Jason and his Argonauts had to end their quest. Jason hat to marry Medea, and the newlyweds had to set sail for a new home in Corinth. Jason hung the Golden Fleece in the temple of Zeus on the way . . . In other words, I had to re-educate myself from my action writer beginnings. In action writing, the climax is always "wham, bam, thank you, ma'am."

Three themes seem apparent to me, after several years of rereading the writings of Campbell, the Bible, Shakespeare, Greek legends, and other literature. Reunion . . .the wedding . . . and flight. I like these ideas. They are really starting to work for me. But, again, you are the writer. It is your story. You know what kind of finish works best for your story. So you have great freedom here . . .

If you are telling an epic war story, you still need a final battle. The battle just isn't as important as your Hero's change. What is important now in a movie like *The Patriot* is simply that Mel Gibson joins the team. If it is a suspense thriller that you are writing, you will still need to sustain your suspense into the climax. You will still probably have a final showdown scene with your Hero and Enemy. But it will be more of a surprise final twist scene, not some gratuitous shoot-out.

The Enemy is acquitted at the trial. The Hero is in the process of "letting go" of his obsession. The Hero has circled back to his romantic interest He has asked her to marry him. They go to the airport. They are leaving for Cancun. The Hero runs into the Enemy there. The Hero discovers the Enemy is using another man's passport. The Hero confronts the Enemy. He discovers something that finally puts all the pieces together. What the Hero chooses to do about his Enemy is not that important. A lot of times the Hero is facing a final choice. Does he bring down the Enemy here and jeopardize his love and marriage? The Hero walks away. He'll take the love and marriage. The ultimate victory here is within his own heart.

REUNION

Reunion with a loved one, reconciliation with a father, a mother, an estranged sibling, has a power that is almost unmatched in storytelling. It also provides symmetry to your Hero's adventure. No matter how extraordinary his struggles, how painful his suffering, he is coming home.

We have mentioned the story of Joseph from the Book of Genesis several times. Joseph as Hero endured years of suffering. He was sold into slavery. He lived as a slave in Egypt for a decade. But Joseph won a great victory. He became the most powerful man in Egypt, second only to the Pharaoh.

But what was the climax of this great adventure? The dramatic narrative led us to a reunion between Joseph and his father, Jacob. Jacob died shortly thereafter. Joseph buried his father in the new land. Joseph had been able to bring his entire family out of the land of starvation and into Egypt. So two elements are present to climax this story, reunion and flight.

BACK TO THE MOVIES

Let's look at a couple of our movies briefly. In *Notting Hill,* Hugh Grant is in the process of letting go. Julia Roberts comes to see him at his bookstore. She finally gets real; she offers him a relationship. But Hugh Grant tells her "No." He tells Roberts that he recognizes that she is a movie star. He is just a "bloke who works in a bookstore." Grant is letting go of his argument that drives him in the movie. Going back to the act of sacrifice, letting go is truly a sacrificial act. Of course, there is a final twist in *Notting Hill.* Grant sits around with his friends discussing his decision. Suddenly, Grant can see by their expressions that maybe he was a little foolish. Grant and his pals make a mad dash to Julia Roberts's press conference. Grant accepts Roberts's offer of a relationship. This is a reunion scene. In this case, it is with the Enemy. But it is still reunion and reconciliation.

In *The Sixth Sense,* we see the process of letting go in two reunion scenes. We have already discussed the goodbye scene between Willis and Haley Joel Osment. Willis and Osment know that the therapist/client relationship is over. It is a sweet, sad scene. The are both letting go . . .

But what are the two final scenes? Osment confronts his mother about the dead people. He has been talking to his dead grandmother. He tells his mother, Toni Colette, that her mother loved her. She did see Colette's dance recital, she simply hid herself in the back. Osment also tells Colette that her mother moved the pendant, not Haley. A flood of emotions overcomes Colette. It is a scene of healing and reconciliation between mother and son. It is also a reunion scene. It allows Toni Colette to have a reunion with her own mother.

Of course, everybody knows the final scene in *The Sixth Sense.* It is what made the movie such a monster hit. Willis's wife is sleeping in front of the television. A video of their wedding is playing on the television. Willis talks to his wife, bringing reconciliation to their hurt feelings. "Why did you leave me?" his wife asks. "I didn't leave you," Willis answers. Then the wife drops the wedding band on the floor. The final twist. Willis realizes he is already dead. Willis begins the process of letting go again. But look at the other elements present in the scene. The wedding. And flight. Willis has to travel now into eternity.

THE WEDDING

Weddings are a classic third act scene. Since the days of Shakespeare, audiences and playwrights understand the need for a celebration, a grand finale. A wedding is truly one of the best celebrations. When Shakespeare wrote a comedy, it usually ended with a wedding. Forget your story for a moment and imagine that you are shooting an MTV video. You shoot some disturbing images, you shoot some sexy images, and then you want to land on some scenes of joy, dancing, happy faces, musicians playing. Love is in the air. Even in these funky, fast-editing videos, you are seeing a story.

Remember audiences have already traveled through a number of trials and tests with your Hero. Now the audience wants some joy. They want hope. If you are writing a comedy, a family drama, whatever, this is a great way to go.

Name the movies? They are too numerous to name. *My Best Friend's Wedding, Runaway Bride*. We just talked about *Notting Hill*. If it is not an actual wedding, a wedding is implicit.

I love a wedding as a final-act celebration. It also allows secondary Heroes to tie up their loose ends during the dancing and celebration. The wedding also operates at a mythic level, a symbolic level. Think of the movie as your Hero's rites of passage. After your Hero has been initiated with trials of fire, he or she is ready to become a full member of the tribe.

FLIGHT

As I have been stressing, these motifs have their genesis in some of our earliest recorded masterpieces of literature.

We discussed the story of Moses. Moses as Hero ultimately led Israel in a flight out of Egypt. The Exodus is a classic Act 3 rising action. Yes, the actual Moses saga continued with the Israel nation's forty years of travails in the desert. Moses, as an old man, still had to come down from the mountain with the Ten Commandments. However, telling this much · story begs the question of three acts. It is more like an eight-hour mini series.

I was not surprised to see that the DreamWorks SKG production team chose to avoid the forty years in the desert. I saw their animated version of Moses in the theaters. I enjoyed it. They concluded their story with . . . you guessed it, the Exodus. The Flight.

How often do you see it? In almost every movie. Let's take a look at our shopping list. In *Notting Hill,* Julia Roberts is on her way to the airport. In *The Sixth Sense* Bruce Willis is leaving for eternity. In *Meet the Parents* Ben Stiller is at the airport, returning to New York. In *The Thomas Crown Affair* Rene Russo is sitting on a plane headed for Europe. Pierce Brosnan is sitting in a seat behind her. How many times have you seen this scene at the end of a movie? The Hero and her new love are sitting on a beach in the Bahamas sipping margaritas. Why do writers keep using these scenes? I think the answer is obvious. Going somewhere symbolizes freedom. It also symbolizes change. Within the confines of the Hero's adventure, our Hero is imprisoned. In the end, we want to see her released from bondage. We want to see her get into the car and head to California. If the movie ends with a wedding, all the better. We know that there is new love, joy for everybody. And our happy couple is about to leave on their honeymoon. The whole thing works symbolically. Every one of us feels imprisoned in some areas of our lives. We yearn for freedom. We dream of flight.

The second explanation is also obvious. We have met the Hero in his or her normal world. We have thrown the Hero into an exotic world. Now we need to let our Hero escape the exotic world. We need to let our Hero return home to his or her normal world. Or we need to let the Hero take a vacation and then build a new normal world, enriched by love. Dorothy needs to get out of Oz. She needs to go home to Kansas. But it should be a new Kansas. She is free now. She is no longer held down by Auntie Em and Miss Gulch.

Dorothy will enroll in some night classes. She will find a man and a career.

HIP ENDINGS

I want to briefly cover a new trend in creating endings. There is a new kind of demand with our final acts. What is hip, cool, and all the rage is to spin the story upside down one more time in the final scene. The Hero drives the story with his argument. He sees his argument defeated by his Enemy, who brings a counter argument. Finally the Hero gains new wisdom and is ready to "win" in the final act with a kind of measured reworked philosophy. Now our hip young writers will completely attack this new wisdom, with a final twist. In other words, we have given the Hero a new argument, a kind of recipe for success. And the final twist is going to blow away this argument. Yet another counter argument.

Bruce Willis in *The Sixth Sense* gradually learns as a child psychologist that he must embrace and "work with" the dead. Of course, what is the final blast against Willis' new perception? Bruce Willis is dead.

The ironic twist factor has become so hip, so expected, so de rigueur in Hollywood, I find it beginning to cripple me as a writer. I find myself abandoning new story lines half way through the process, because I can't envision some shocking, mind blowing, audience-numbing final spin.

Listen, if Alex Lasker and I were adapting *Firefox* now, we would probably be bantering around this concept with Eastwood in his office. What would be the final spin for Eastwood's pilot as he flies the super plane home? He is winning. His damaged psyche has not folded under pressure. He has stolen the plane. He has healed his inner conflict. So, what now?

As today's writers, we would now pull back and see that Eastwood is sitting in front of a large television monitor. He is playing a video game called "Super Pilot." He is still damaged. He hears a chopper overhead, and crawls under his desk in fear. He is still in Alaska. He has never left his house.

Look, there is a precedent for this kind of climax irony. Travel back five thousand years to the Book of Job. After all of the horror that Job endured the loss of his sons and daughters, the loss of his home and his possessions, the loss of his wife, the boils and plagues; what then? Job discovered that God and Satan were just waging a little friendly bet, "Let's test Job and see if he will lose his faith . . . I was just testing you, Job. You are okay now. I am going to give everything back."

I think you get the drift. But what is my point here? Don't get hung up on this. Tell a good story. Create a satisfying ending. Some stories don't need the hip ending.

FINAL THOUGHTS

So, let's return to our discussion of more traditional endings. Early on, I talked about my discussion with my story analyst friend at Disney. I talked about how we simplified script plotting. "The first act is the Hero's argument. The second act is all of the arguments against them. And the third act is the author's argument". The death scene with your Hero and his scenes of suffering serve to teach your Hero. He or she needs to let go of one way of thinking. Sometimes he has to let go of both ways of thinking. In your final act, your Hero generally needs a reunion with his Enemy, or a loved one. Here he is letting go again. Then, as a final surprise, the Hero can find what he is looking for. The very act of letting go now allows the Hero to obtain what he wanted the whole time. This is the Author's Argument. Your Argument. It is nothing big. It is simple.

Going back to *Meet the Parents,* Ben Stiller leaves Teri Polo and her family and heads to the airport. He is letting go. He is letting go of his way of thinking that he can marry the princess bride without growing up. And he is letting go of his inner conflict, his low self-esteem. But the process of letting go provides Stiller with a pleasurable surprise. He experiences two final reunions, first with DeNiro. It is a scene of negotiation and reconciliation. Then with Teri Polo. They reconcile. He is allowed to marry Teri Polo after all.

I want to mention a sweet movie, *Where the Heart Is,* with Natalie Portman and Ashley Judd. The screenplay was written by Lowell Ganz and Babaloo Mandel, one of the most successful duos in town. I mention it in passing because it isn't one of the movies that I would normally suggest you rent. The crux of the movie is that Natalie Portman and Ashley Judd suffer a similar wound. They both fall for the wrong kind of man. They have babies with these men and the men leave them. Natalie Portman is left pregnant in the parking lot of a Wal-Mart. She sleeps in the Wal-Mart and has the baby in a frightening scene on the floor of the store. I discussed this movie in a recent screenwriting class. This birth scene is one of the most effective first act "jolts" that I have seen in recent years.

The movie details Portman and Judd and their growing pains together. Portman meets James Frain. He is a nice man. She cannot return his love. How does the inner conflict play out for Portman? She cannot make the jump in the attraction department. She is too used to the bad boys in tight jeans and T-shirts. Ashley Judd must grow up first. Her growth comes as a result of a number of bad relationships and physical abuse. She teaches Portman through her negative experiences, first and foremost. But Judd also teaches through the dialogue. She tells Portman that she should go for it with Frain. "You love him," she says, "why don't you tell him?" Portman has the opportunity but cannot bring herself to say it.

Portman has a goal in this story, it is her argument. She is trying to create a new life in Oklahoma. She wants to love again. But the old tapes keep getting in the way. Portman's mother abandoned her when she was young. Her boyfriend abandoned her at the Wal-Mart. Portman is used to abandonment. James Frain is a loving, sensitive guy. Portman doesn't know what to do with him.

What is the climax of this movie? Portman takes flight. She leaves Oklahoma in search of Frain. But first she stops at a hospital. It is a reunion scene with her old boyfriend, the father of her child. Dylan Bruno has lost his legs in a train accident. He apologizes to her and he tells her that he ran from her because he was afraid. He wishes for the opportunity to make it right. This is a reunion scene with the Enemy. He is teaching Portman, too. Portman finds Frain in Maine on a college campus. Portman has a chance to make it right. She says, "I love you." This is the second reunion.

What is the final scene? You guessed it. It is a wedding scene in Oklahoma. Natalie Portman gets married.

THE PERFECT MOVIE

Even in a brilliant tragic vision like Oliver Stone's *Platoon,* the final moments are still Flight. Most of the platoon is dead. The war in the bush has degenerated into senseless slaughter on both sides. Charlie Sheen has killed Berenger in revenge. Sheen climbs on the Freedom Bird to go home. He is battered and broken. But he is going home. Willem Dafoe is trying desperately to reach the plane. He is shot down by the Enemy. He has been betrayed by Berenger. He raises his arms like Christ on the cross. He is Messianic. He will "take flight" as a saint.

CHAPTER 19

GOOD NEWS/BAD NEWS

Okay, you and your partner are sitting down at your kitchen table. You have your stack of note cards, and you have my model placed in the middle of your table. You have figured out your Hero and you have come up with a really good Enemy. You have an overall idea of the story you want to tell. You guys are talking together, you have some chips, some Danish, coffee and Cokes. You have already figured out a couple of your big engagement or battle scenes. The scenes are good, they have a good jolt to them, a good shift or a twist. But I know what you are thinking, "What about the scenes in between?"

The bottom line is that this is your story. You are free to go anywhere you wish with your story. Use the model if you need it. You may not need it at all. You may have so many rich and challenging characters, and so many outrageous scenes planned, that you will find your own structure. That is great. Just remember that your Hero has to "fall."

I am going to offer you and important trick that the pros use. Yes. No. Yes. No. Or, as they refer to it around Hollywood, Good News/Bad News. Good News/Bad News. For some reason this is taboo. Nobody admits to it. But everybody uses it. This is a classic pro trick. It will help get you through.

Hey, this is the fun of screenwriting. This puts fun into your plotting. You and your partner begin to think of these Good News/Bad News reversals and sometimes, they will make you laugh out loud. And you haven't even written the scenes yet. This is the scheme the pros use. Listen, some screenwriters, especially comedy writers, will refer to this technique as reversals. I call them reversals much of the time. But Good News/Bad News is a specific kind of reversal. This term works when I am talking about a sequence of scenes. There is a flood of new ensemble multi-plot action/comedies. *Pulp Fiction, Happiness, Go,* on and on. These young writers are using this device almost exclusively. Setup. Pay off. Good News. Bad News. Big huge reversals within a scene. In *Pulp Fiction,* John Travolta is assigned to protect his mob boss's girlfriend. Travolta decides to turn it into a date. The chemistry is there. Travolta really turns on the charm with Uma Thurman. For Travolta, this is Good News. They have fun. Then she overdoses on him. Bad News. Travolta learns his lesson. This is MTV, short attention span storytelling.

In *Meet the Parents,* let's do a quick study of Good News/Bad News. Ben Stiller and his fiancé, Teri Polo meet the parents Robert DeNiro and Blythe Danner. DeNiro likes the green color of Stiller's car. Good News . . . But, DeNiro is immediately doing "twenty questions" on Stiller. "Do you like cats?" Teri Polo blurts out, "He doesn't like cats." Bad News. DeNiro probes Stiller on his profession, "Are you really a nurse?" Bad news. DeNiro is a macho army, CIA guy.

DeNiro invites Stiller to ride into town with him. They agree on Peter, Paul and Mary's "Puff the Magic Dragon." Good song. Male bonding. Good News. But Stiller doesn't know when to quit. He starts claiming that "Puff the Magic Dragon" is really about being high on marijuana. Bad decision. Bad News. This creates the comedy. This is also the fun of writing.

A lot of the young hot writers and directors in Hollywood use this device. It drives their movies and it drives the comedy. They will use reversals within a single scene. Using reversals within a scene is standard operating procedure these days for comic effect. I remember a particular episode of *Sex and the City* where Kim Catrell decided she was going to try and meet a different kind of man. A suit and tie kind of guy. She meets him; he is sitting at a bar, it is a blind date. He immediately starts talking sexy to her, bragging about his bedsmanship. He is very aggressive. He suggests they go home together that night. Kim Catrell is excited, her face is flushed. She says "yes." He stands up to go to the men's room. He is only five feet, four inches tall! Kim Catrell's jaw drops to the floor. It is a great reversal within the scene. It is funny. For Kim Catrell, it is Good News/Bad News.

CHAPTER 20

THE MAGIC "3": DO IT IN THREES

Some of you may have heard of this axiom tossed around, maybe in a writing class, or somewhere. It is a cliché and most Hollywood writers know it, but nobody explains it. What it means is, if you have a unique idea that you are using, or an interesting character, the idea or the character needs to appear at three different points in your story to be effective.

It also applies to . . . DECISIONS.

This is one of the hidden secrets that you can learn right off the top . . . right now! It should shape your plot line no matter if you are writing a comedy, a love story, or an action adventure, whatever . . .

We must see your Hero make at least three bad decisions. Then, at the end of Act 2, the Hero "gets it right," and makes one good decision. This helps him/her win in Act 3 . . . This is how movies work.

Now some major movies will use two major bad decisions and then one good decision in Act 3 . . . Still the magic "3." Remember that Hollywood always chooses to discuss screenplays in terms of "3" Acts, so:

Act 1   Hero makes a bad decision
Act 2   Hero makes a bad decision
Act 3   Hero makes a good decision
The magic "3."

BUT, generally, in today's hip, character-driven movies, I usually can count "3" bad decisions before a good decision. Sometimes more than three.

How do you teach yourself? Simple, do what I do:

1. Rent three videos that we have discussed in this book.
2. Watch them and try to spot the big bad decisions the Hero makes.
3. Write them down: Three movies, three columns, side by side as follows:

Movie 1	Movie 2	Movie 3
Bad decision	Bad decision	Bad decision
Bad decision	Bad decision	Bad decision
Bad decision	Bad decision	Bad decision
Good decision	Good decision	Good decision

They are usually simple. But each will shape all the plotting for the next twenty minutes of film time.

After you have spent one or two nights of movie watching, you will be ready to plot your story. Keep this flow sheet right beside you as a guide. Don't steal from these movies; create your own story. But the flow sheets will be your reminder as you begin to plot.

I will finish with an example of Bad decision/Good decision from one of our movies.

Take a look at David O'Williams's *Three Kings* with George Clooney and Mark Wahlberg.

Our American heroes are in the Persian Gulf. They find a cache of gold and decide to take it home with them. The "spoils of war." Bad decision.

Our Heroes run into a group of innocent Iraqis who are victims of torture and murder at the hands of the Republican Guard. George Clooney watches a mother executed. He wants to help. A Republican guard gives Clooney a choice. Our Heroes have the gold in the truck. They can go, or they can stay and try to be Heroes. Clooney and Wahlberg choose to go. They take the gold. Second bad decision. In the middle of the movie, Wahlberg is kidnapped by the Republican guard. Clooney and his friends must team up with the innocent Iraqi people. Clooney is still negotiating to keep the gold. Third bad decision. By the end of the movie, they must discover their humanity. Our Heroes begin to see the light: not to indulge their amoral needs.

You wouldn't believe how many screenplays I've read where the Hero travels through eighty or ninety pages on only one decision. It becomes redundant, boring. Movies need "The Magic 3."

CHAPTER 21

YOU ARE THE TRUTH

Find your own story. That is the most important thing. If you can tell it to your friends at a restaurant, you are there. If you can see it, if you know it as a complete idea, if it moves you, you are there. If you can pose it as a question, if you can answer it with three separate support ideas, you are there. You may not need all of these techniques, or tricks, or story sections. You may not need to agonize over plot shifts, or finding a "belly of the beast" experience. Your story will offer you the experiences.

Think of this book as a piano lesson. Your instructor sits down with you and makes you practice scales. He has a metronome sitting there, ticking back and forth. That is what all of these techniques and ideas are, just musical scales and a metronome. The child prodigy ignores the scales immediately, and starts playing the classics at six years old. But even the rest of us grow weary of scales very quickly. We grab a tune that we like and we learn to play. We practice it over and over, until we are really good at it. Then we want to play it in front of an audience.

Find your story and begin working on it. Keep working on it. If one section of your story is a problem, maybe you go back to the scales for a couple of minutes. Maybe you will find something in this book that helps you; but you always return to your tune. You keep playing it over and over, until you are really good at it. Then you find an audience.

If you have an idea, it is everything. If you have a great story, you have gold. You will find a way to make it work.

Most of us tried to learn to play guitar at one time. We took lessons at the guitar shop. They insisted that we learn to read music. They taught us to play folk tunes, and play with our fingers. But one day at home, we figured out the riff to "Stairway to Heaven." We were off and running. If you find your story, it is your "Stairway to Heaven." So start writing.

I have a friend who was browsing around in a used bookstore. He found a book that was interesting and out of print. He tracked down the owner. He talked the author into an option for one year for one dollar. My friend fashioned a screenplay out of the book. He sold it. It became a movie, *Escape from Alcatraz*. He now has a major career as a screenwriter. I have another friend who was arrested in the airport of a Middle-Eastern country. He wrote a book about his experiences. It became a movie, *Midnight Express*. If you find your story, you are there. Keep writing until it is great. Then play it in front of an audience. You can and will do it.

I started writing in the post-Vietnam era in the early eighties. Humanism, the "me" generation, and intellectual cynicism dominated the landscape. I grew up the son of a Protestant minister. My father wasn't a hellfire and brimstone type. In fact, he was quite the opposite. He was a life-loving optimist. He was one of the first ministers to allow a rock band to play in his church. But the point is, I felt embarrassed about my roots. I thought that nobody in Hollywood would care. In the eighties in Hollywood, I thought that writing about God and Midwestern preachers or characters that had conflicts of conscious was politically incorrect. I was wrong.

I look back on those days and I am embarrassed at my own fear. Never let Hollywood impose their value system on you. You are the artist. Your philosophy, your value system is your truth. You are the truth.

I now embrace my roots. I miss my father and his faith. Your family background, the profound conflict that resonates in you as a child or adolescent is gold. No matter how funky, or sad, or uninteresting you think your story is, it is your strength. It is your specialness. Celebrate it. Weave it into the fabric of your story. This is your power.

INDEX

C

WENDELL WELLMAN

Wendell Wellman is a professional screenwriter who has worked on many successful films with high profile producers. His first work to hit the big screen was Clint Eastwood's *Firefox,* and he has written for Mr. Eastwood on other films, including *Sudden Impact.* He has recently finished a new screenplay, *ID,* and has several other scripts in development. Wendell has also just completed a new book, *A Writer's Road Map.*

Besides being a successful writer, Mr. Wellman is an accomplished actor who has worked in film, television, and theater for more than a decade. His work includes memorable roles in the films *Sudden Impact, Somersby, Curfew,* and *Streets of Dreams.* Mr. Wellman has worked with Clint Eastwood, Richard Gere, Jodie Foster, Bill Pullman, Morgan Fairchild, Lee Marvin, and many others. He founded the West End Theater Company, an acclaimed professional group in Los Angeles, which has produced major plays, several of which Mr. Wellman wrote and starred in.

Wendell received his M.A. in English Literature from UCLA, and taught at UCLA's Extension classes for five years. He has taught at The Learning Annex, is a repeat guest lecturer with Sony Studios's "Story-board Group," and teaches professional classes within his theater.

Printed in the United States
971200001B